to
Cate
in honor of the
gift of your Body.

blessings

Jeanne

RECLAIMING THE AUTHENTIC SELF

RECLAIMING
THE AUTHENTIC SELF

By

Dianne Lancaster

4·Sight Press Inc.
Boulder, Colorado

RECLAIMING THE AUTHENTIC SELF
4•Sight Press Inc. / October 1996

Copyright © 1996 by Dianne Lancaster.
With *Soul Engagements* by Marily Charles.
Cover design and book layout by Conde Freeman.
First printing 1996.

Library of Congress Cataloging-in-Publication Data:
Lancaster, Dianne
    Reclaiming the Authentic Self / by Dianne Lancaster
    ISBN 0-9655069-4-0
    1. Self-Actualization/Self-Help
    1996
                        96-090739
                        CIP

Published in the United States

4•Sight Press Inc.
P. O. Box 1488, Boulder, CO 80306-1488

Printed in the United States

To Diane Cook,
the most extraordinary human being
I have ever known.

IN APPRECIATION

 For everyone who has participated in this program — from its inception in 1980 to those who joined us during the summer of 1996 — thank you for calling forth this information. It has given meaning to my life, purpose to my teaching, and inspiration to face the challenges it offers to all who seek change.

I made it to this point in my life, however, with the love and support of a few very special, dedicated souls.

To Diane Cook and Melissa Michaels I offer my profound gratitude. You, more than anyone, know the challenges that made this book possible. And you, more than anyone, gave me the support and courage to express my Authentic Self.

To Kitty Macario and Barbara Barnes I say, once again, thank you for helping me survive Washington, D.C. I could not have done this lifetime without you.

To Maria Benning, whose devotion to these principles is continually inspiring, I add my thank you for editing, proofing, assembling and overseeing the gathering of these words into print.

And to Conde Freeman, designer extraordinaire, thank you so much for this inspiring book cover, for the tireless hours of layout design, and for your willingness to support this project under the intense circumstances and deadline.

To those whose dedication to getting this book into print made it all possible, my thankfulness is boundless. To Kathleen Hammond, whose "Let's go for it!" inspired me to do so, thank you for the love and understanding that helped the barriers dissolve.

To Susan Peguero who transcribed, edited, and encouraged, thank you for embodying and reflecting the life-changing principles this book contains. To Donna Chimera, a great soul and truly gifted writer, thank you for helping to navigate this project into publication, and for encouraging so many others to experience this program.

Thank you Marily Charles, for the model of reclaiming your power, and for sharing your vibrant creativity as a rich complement to this writing. Thank you Linda Wolf, not only for supporting this project, but also for committing to this program so earnestly and inspiringly. Thank you Dorian Weatherley-White for supporting this teaching, and for your courageous application of the "Women, Power, Money and Love" principles.

Thank you Sally Adams, for bringing together so many essential resources. And thank you Carol Hoskins for taking care of details so that I could keep commitments and stay focused.

Thanks also to Channah Adler — for your support in my life, my work, my teaching and my Being.

Thank you Kathleen Martin and Karen Sharp for your continued commitment to this work. Thank you Brook Jasmyn for your encouragement and confirmation, and also for modeling the power of the gifted teacher.

Thank you Jacquelyn Small, for inspiring my personal growth, and for acknowledging and supporting my writing and teaching.

Thanks also to the little brothers whose love is with me every day.

And although you have heard it a hundred times, thank you again, Warren Bellows — my colleague, teacher, friend, healer and fellow traveler in the dimensions we call home.

CONTENTS

It is necessary for

the salvation of man

that certain truths which

exceed human reason

should be made

known to him

by divine revelation.

— *St. Thomas Aquinas*

FROM THE AUTHOR

Everything I know, and all that I am, lasered into my consciousness when, in August 1976, I had what is written in the literature as the Experience of Cosmic Consciousness. That series of multidimensional revelations began with the room filling with an incredible deep, pink light, and with that light there was a message being conveyed to me: that I was going to amount to something. Because my family had always told me the opposite, my response was, no, I'll never amount to anything. But the light stayed, and the message was insistent. Some of my life flashed before me — my childhood, a failed marriage, numerous self-destructive feats — and I was certain that this type of person was indeed worthless. Nevertheless, the light remained, and so did the conveyance, insisting that I had a value, a purpose, a mission to fulfill.

As if to convince me that I was not the hopeless, lost soul I felt I was, I was then shown every moment of this lifetime, all at once; and as if that were not awesome enough, right beside each moment I was shown the purpose of each of those moments . . . and I wept, profoundly. I had not even know there *was* a purpose for anything, much less my own catastrophic life. To be shown that the purpose of the conditions in my life had been to prepare me to teach others how to reverse and recover from similarly debilitating conditions was an incredibly inspiring, healing experience . . . to be followed by much, much more, I immediately discovered.

The Other Dimensions

With my consciousness already suspended from ordinary reality, I next watched all the energy in this universe configure in a manner that I was to understand was the fourth dimension. Then all the energy reconfigured and was shown to me as the fifth dimension. Then the sixth dimension; the seventh; the eighth; the ninth . . . and that, I was to understand, was the edge of human consciousness. My own consciousness then changed so that I was not merely seeing the different energy patterns of the different dimensions; suddenly I was in the ninth dimension, in the energy of what we frequently refer to as God. I not only saw everything that is, or has been, or will be. I *was* everything. I was the energy of each atom, molecule, dust speck, grain of sand, caterpillar, mountain, thought and word. I knew everything that was known now, everything that had ever been known, and everything that ever would be known.

I also saw the evolutionary plan for it all — everything that ever had been, everything that is being at any given moment, and everything that ever will be. I saw the evolutionary plan for all levels of consciousness: leaves, plastic, glass, tires, insects, humans, buildings, corporations. I saw all the levels of human evolution like an enormous matrix: a gigantic Rubik cube with a matrix within each of its cubes; and yet another matrix within each of those cubes; and matrix-to-cube-to-matrix-to-cube-to-matrix-to-cube *ad infinitum.*

I was shown how many billions of universes there are, and how moderately evolved this one is. I watched energy enter this universe from the one "below" us, and I saw the macro-consciousness that was assigned at that moment to that tiniest particle of energy, designating everything it ever will be, and appropriating at that moment all the energy it ever will take for that particle to be all of those possibilities. Simultaneously I saw energy that had reached its highest potential in this universe's evolutionary plan go out of this universe and into the next, more "evolved" universe.

From that ninth dimensional consciousness that knows everything, I went into the eighth dimension, which knows absolutely nothing. It is only energy — shown to me as silvery-gray. But since the entirety of the ninth dimension is consumed by knowing, it cannot cause anything to occur. That requires energy. Anything that is to occur must first be conceived in that ninth dimension. But that consciousness which only *knows* must be combined with the energy in the eighth dimension in order for something to occur. And that is the seventh dimension, which was shown to me as tiny gold scrolls. That is where everything that ever will be, plus the energy to enable it to happen, are merged.

The sixth dimension is the energy from the seventh dimension released one moment at a time. Thus, even though everything that ever will be has been thought of in the ninth dimension, and even though the energy to ensure it happens has been allocated from the eighth dimension and reserved in the seventh, to create one moment at a time on Planet Earth, the sixth dimension releases its energy.

The fifth dimension was shown to be the bi-polar consciousness of the soul. From all of the energy released from the sixth dimension to create a moment on Earth, the soul distinguishes which of that energy is directed specifically to it. The fifth dimension also contains information relative to the purpose of energy being allocated to each separate soul. Since the primary function of the soul is to oversee simultaneously the evolution of the three levels of human consciousness — ego, subconscious and unconscious — as the soul interprets the energy from the sixth dimension, and the purpose that energy is to serve in the evolution of human consciousness, the soul directs that energy accordingly in relation to the purpose each moment is to serve in the evolution of one of the three levels of human consciousness.

The fourth dimension is the consciousness of the soul, and to understand it I was taken into the energy of the collective soul. From that perspective, I understood that the soul is humanity's vibrational link to the creator consciousness: the consciousness that is the ninth dimension. I was shown that truth is the word humanity uses to describe the quality of information communicated from the God consciousness; that the soul is humanity's source of truth; and that intuition is the soul's communication link with the human ego. Accordingly, truth is the energy, or information, by which human consciousness evolves.

From there I was taken into the collective consciousness of the human ego, the third dimension of consciousness. Then into the second dimension of consciousness, the human subconscious, and then into the first dimension of consciousness, the human unconscious. I was shown that they each have a purpose in relation to truth. The unconscious blocks truth, the subconscious stores truth and the ego interprets and expresses truth . . . except, that is, for the fact that because the ego is still evolving in its relationship with truth, it does have access to doubt and denial, which are the ego's most formidable weapons against truth.

Following this extensive foray into the dimensions of human consciousness, I returned to the seventh dimension to understand how the soul interacts with and contributes to the evolution of the three levels of consciousness assigned to humanity. What I was shown is that in between lifetimes the soul meets with the "Divine Planning Committee" to preview the next lifetime it is to oversee. In that process, the soul appears in front of a series of bins. Each bin contains the energy of various components of life on Earth: health, parents, education, money, career, relationships, etc. As the soul is presented to one of those bins — health, for example — energy is disbursed from it. That is the energy to create the quality of health of the ego the soul will be overseeing the next lifetime. At the same time that energy is released from the bin, the soul gets a macro-conscious understanding of what the health of the ego it oversees next will be like.

Then the soul goes to the next bin. Parents, for example. The Divine Planning Committee releases from that bin a certain quality and quantity of energy and the soul previews what the ego's relationship with the parents will be like. From this dimension the soul continues to interact with energies to be allocated onto the Earth plane to create the next lifetime it is to oversee.

In this manner, the soul does have an idea of what the karmic issues of the next lifetime will include. When almost no energy is disbursed from the career bin, the ego will have few issues with career. This could be a lifetime wherein a factory worker is at the same job the entire lifetime, obtaining periodic raises, pension contributions, vacations and sick leave, etc.

Once those seventh dimension energies have been allocated, they are then transferred onto the Earth plane and become the human unconscious. In that role, those energies gradually unfold throughout the lifetime to accomplish the lessons the ego has been assigned for its next evolutionary venture: the next lifetime. For this reason, the energies remain unconscious throughout the lifetime. They are purposely so.

If the ego knew at one time all the lessons it was to experience, the ego's consciousness would be enlightened and it would not have lessons. It would know everything. The purpose of the unconscious, therefore, is to release the energy to produce the lessons that comprise the lifetime in accordance with the divine plan of consciousness evolution.

The subconscious, on the other hand, is created in the immediate lifetime. It is a consciousness of all the experiences the ego has in a given lifetime. It is a "sub" consciousness, however, because it is both unnecessary and impossible for the ego to hold in its consciousness each moment an awareness of everything that has ever passed through its consciousness up until that moment.

As it is, once something passes through the ego's consciousness, that information is stored below the surface of the ego's consciousness, subject to retrieval. When the ego loses its car keys, for example, it will eventually rely on the subconscious to help it retrace its activities and remember that the keys were left in the front door. In the meantime, however, the subconscious may have offered up its "logical" information as well: they could be in the briefcase, on the kitchen counter, between the sofa cushions, in a coat pocket . . . etc.

The Master Teachers

After this understanding of the evolution of human consciousness I was then shown a diamond-shaped image.

To the left was the Buddha, and I was absorbed into his energies and teachings. At the bottom of the diamond was the Prophet Mohammed. I was likewise absorbed into his energies and teachings. To the right side of the diamond was the master teacher Christ. I was absorbed into his energies and teachings, as well. And at the top of the diamond was a woman whom I did not recognize; but as I was absorbed into her energies and teachings I became aware that she is the master teacher for the Aquarian Age.

Twelve Gold Pyramids

Next there appeared before me twelve gold pyramids. As I looked at the first one, the top of it opened and a gold laser beam came into my forehead, into the area I now know is the sixth chakra, the third eye. Then the contents of that pyramid came down the gold laser beam and were emptied into my third eye: books, gemstones, gold coins — incredible valuables pouring into my consciousness.

Then the top of the second pyramid opened. A gold laser beam came to my third eye, and the contents of that pyramid emptied into my consciousness. Then the next, and the next, until all twelve pyramids had emptied their contents onto a gold laser beam and into my consciousness.

From there I was taken into a gigantic room (which I now know was the Akashic Records) with twelve huge, towering arched columns of wisdom. I was in the center of the room on a tiny, tiny pedestal, and one by one each of the columns came crashing down onto me — and yet, even though I expected to be crushed by each of them, I was not.

Then to my left an enormous gold throne appeared. It was unoccupied, yet I knew to go up the three steps leading to it and kneel. As I did so, a gold sword appeared. It touched my right shoulder, arched over my head and touched my left shoulder, then over my head again, touching my right shoulder.

Sometime during the course of this experience I was taken back to LeMuria, the era before Atlantis, when the unconscious was formed.

The LeMurian Era

Everything about LeMuria was shown to me in a sepia color because the rods and cones of the human eye had not been formed at that time.

What was most startling about that era, however, was how non-complex life on Earth was. So much so that everything was "heard" more than seen. The vibration of a mountain was heard. A rock was heard. In fact, in a manner similar to hearing the Music of the Spheres (which I did hear that August afternoon), one moment at a time on Earth could be heard all at once.

The reason the vibration of each living and non-living thing was so important is that LeMuria was the beginning of humanity's development of senses — and the two senses related to that era were hearing and smell. The principal sense was hearing; thus, every thing was experienced through its vibration being heard. The sense of hearing was also humanity's source of information for safety and protection. And the secondary sense developed in LeMuria was smell.

The elephant, with its enormous ears, is the animal kingdom's carryover from LeMuria. During that era, a sign of status came from placing gemstones in the ears of the elephants that were a part of one's "tribe." That ritual has carried over in humanity's consciousness and now is experienced as ear piercing.

Because humanity's unconscious was developed in LeMuria, life was quite rote-like. (A present-day legacy of LeMurian karma is humanity's resistance to change.) Without a subconscious to produce dynamics such as forgetting, or comparisons, life in LeMuria simply "was." Until, that is, the first emotion developed.

Fear set in when the winds came. In fact, LeMuria was destroyed by winds. Not until the unconscious had been fully developed, however. But, because the unconscious was not sufficiently evolved to accommodate the addition of the next level of consciousness, the subconscious, all the energy of LeMuria was "destroyed" — taken back into the cosmos. There it was recalibrated and returned to the Earth plane as Atlantis.

The Atlantean Era

The principal sense developed in this era was taste; the secondary sense was touch. Eating disorders, addictions, sexual abuse . . . they are all legacies of Atlantean karma.

Hierarchies, systems, energy and time awareness — they, too, come from Atlantis. Watches are also from Atlantis. The main karmic issue from Atlantis, however, is values. Ethics. Integrity. Honesty. Doing the right thing. These, and abuses of them, are classic karma from the Atlantean era.

The color gray is also Atlantean. Thus, if someone is wearing gray the first time you meet, you can know that your relationship with that person is from the Atlantean era. If a person is wearing brown when you first meet, that is LeMurian. Individuals who wear tan and other anemic shades of brown are often reflecting their relationship with fear. And often, individuals who wear black predominantly are going through a period, or perhaps a lifetime, of burning through Atlantean karma with anger. The anger developed when Atlantis was "destroyed." Having hosted the development of a subconscious, the era of Atlantis enabled humanity to store information. Ultimately, the capacity to store information led to the inclination to use it . . . and not necessarily for the good of human kind.

Issues of control and the abuse of power emerged from Atlantis. As a result, anger developed in reaction to the control. Control of information was an especially prickly issue in Atlantis — one that is being played out rather prominently in today's computer-based technology and information storage/retrieval systems. The anger epidemic on this planet is also a carryover from Atlantis, with the inequitable distribution of resources at its root.

As the symbology from dreams signifies, water represents the subconscious; and when water "destroyed" Atlantis, it was because the subconscious had been saturated with information it did not know how to use.

"Information overload" is the modern-day term. And clearly, one of humanity's most pressing karmic issues from Atlantis is in information discrimination. From junk mail and suspicion of the news media to disinformation, virtual reality and the government's "plausible deniability" routines . . . the subconscious unable to distinguish truth is a disturbing karmic issue to be played out in the coming years.

The Universal Era

When Atlantis was "destroyed," its energy was returned to the cosmos, calibrated to accommodate the addition of the ego, and all of that energy returned to create the current era, which will ultimately be labeled the Universal era. During its tenure, the primary sense that has been developed is the fifth sense, sight. The secondary sense humanity is developing this era is the sixth, to know. The seventh sense, to Be, will be manifested in the next age, Aquarius; as will the eighth sense, to co-create simultaneously with the God consciousness.

To comprehend the ninth sense, to Be One with that God consciousness, is outside the boundaries of human consciousness.

What is well within those boundaries is the consciousness of the soul, the next level of consciousness that is being added to humanity's experience of life on Earth. And what is unprecedented is that the next level of consciousness is being added while the others remain in place.

The unconscious was not sufficiently evolved to accommodate the addition of the subconscious, so LeMuria was "destroyed" and returned as Atlantis. The subconscious was not sufficiently evolved to accommodate the addition of the ego, so Atlantis was "destroyed" and all of its energy reconvened to create the current, Universal, era. The ego is, however, sufficiently evolved to accommodate the presence and merger of the soul — but just barely, as we are finding out.

As the bearer of truth, the soul is waging a veritable war with the ego — and that is the crisis in consciousness humanity is currently undergoing. The entirety of the planet will certainly not have to be blown up in order to halt the ego's recklessness. However, because the ego has used its considerable creativity to amass such destructive capabilities, the fusion of the fourth and third dimensions of human consciousness will precipitate a number of challenging developments before the ego finally yields to the soul's guidance.

The Next Age: Aquarius

Following forays into the two previous eras, as well as an extensive briefing relative to the current era, I was taken into the next era following this one, the Age of Aquarius. I was shown that in that next era, humanity will have only two levels of consciousness, the ego and the soul. Therefore, the principal challenge of this current era, wherein the ego is being developed, is to illuminate and eliminate the subconscious and unconscious patterns that obstruct the ego's relationship with truth.

The primary reason for this is to prepare humanity for the profound experience of love that the next Age will bring. Thus, because love is humanity's emotional reward for its relationship with truth, the quality and quantity of truth in one's life affects the quality and quantity of love. Lower consciousness patterns obstructing one's relationship with truth/love must be eliminated in order for humanity to experience the unconditional divine love that the next Age will bring.

The Times Ahead

In connection with that dismantling of humanity's subconscious and unconsciousness, I was shown that there would be intense struggles on this planet, principally because institutions, bureaucracies, governments, value systems — anything created to harbor those lower consciousness patterns — would be targeted for transformation so that their energies could be reallocated. In essence, I was shown the redistribution of power and wealth on the planet that was to occur during the decade of the 1990s — and I was shown how certain conditions in place in the 1980s would be a warning of the consequences that the various imbalances and indulgences would produce.

For example, I was shown a slate-colored sky, which I knew to be some kind of environmental threat, but the term "greenhouse effect" had not been introduced yet, so I leaped to the conclusion that nuclear war was inevitable. I was assured that that was not the case; that even though humanity had accumulated both the munitions to destroy itself, as well as the emotional volatility, the human ego would not be given the power to destroy itself and an entire sister planet in the solar system.

What I was shown, however, is that there would clearly be difficult times ahead: financial and economic turbulence, food shortages, power outages, drought and floods, terrorism, disease, riots — and although I did not understand it at the time, I was shown virtual reality, errors in databases, disinformation and, as a result, a desperate struggle to find truth in the midst of information that was useless, unreliable, mismanaged and abused.

At the same time, I was assured that there would be enough resources for humanity to survive these difficult times, primarily because whatever had been targeted for transformation would release the energy for rebuilding to occur, almost simultaneously. In other words, the rebuilding and the dismantling would be occurring at the same time. The fourth dimensional redistribution of power and wealth ensures that the energy of corrupt, self-serving systems that are dismantled will go up into the cosmos; that energy will be neutralized so that it can never again be used to serve the ego; then it will be reallocated onto the Earth plane to create communities, governments, economies and value systems that will provide the greatest good for the greatest number.

The most important aspect of this plan is for individuals to be prepared to steward, not control, the resources to build the future. Those resources will be accessible and plentiful, but they do have a different energy — and they have a different purpose — from the energy and resources that have created what we are presently hosting on this planet. Hierarchies built on exploitation, personal fortunes amassed through greed, monuments to ego-based power — these are on the way out. Energies to build the future are stored in the fourth dimension, where the soul has dominion. Based on an individual's qualities — truth, integrity, courage, accountability — energies from that dimension will be released for the individual to steward the energies and resources in accordance with their purpose.

Future Money

In specific, the energy of future money knows where it is to be; it knows how it is to serve; and it cannot be manipulated or controlled by an insecure, greedy, self-serving ego. It is incumbent on individuals to listen to the money and steward it in accordance with its purpose. To do otherwise will compromise one's relationship with money: the money will vacate that individual's presence and move on to the presence of someone who is willing to steward the money so that it accomplishes its purpose. In other words, in the redistribution of power and wealth, the universal consciousness will allocate adequate resources to create the future in accordance with the divine plan — not the ego's will. The human ego does not have the capacity to figure out how to unravel certain of the conditions that have amassed on this planet. The divine plan will accomplish that. However, the ego must not interfere with that plan. The ego either cooperates or it will not be included.

The universal, God/creator consciousness does not operate in the third dimension of human consciousness. It is a ninth dimension consciousness. It relies, therefore, on the ego to distribute resources on the third dimension. That God consciousness has its emissary, however. The soul is its representative. An ego that is willing to follow soul guidance will therefore be utilized in the redistribution of resources. That individual's relationship with truth will ensure it has all the love it needs, and all the security it needs; therefore, it can be entrusted with the money and resources. That individual does not *need* the money or resources because the love that is within is all that is needed. Thus, however the universal consciousness directs the resources to be allocated, that individual will comply without hesitation.

The resources to create the future are to be stewarded, not controlled. They are to serve the collective, not the ego. And once this redistribution has been fulfilled, the karmic system will have served its purpose. Humanity will have reversed the consequences accumulated through the ego's infidelity to truth, as the term "truth *or* consequences" implies, and humanity's manifest destiny of love, security, abundance and peace will be on Earth.

Oversouls and Agents

In the meantime, there is a lot of work to do, and this book is dedicated to some of those who will do the work . . . devoted, gifted souls whom I am to refer to as Aquarian Agents™. The "TM" after this terms means that it is a specific term. It refers to individuals whose soul vibration had passed through the karmic system and was on duty in the Aquarian Age when a crisis of consciousness of unprecedented proportions developed on Planet Earth.

That crisis relates to the merger of ego and soul — ego and truth.

Whereas LeMuria had to be "destroyed" and its energy reconvened as Atlantis — and whereas Atlantis was "destroyed" and its energies returned to create the current Universal era — the Divine Plan assures us that we will not have to destroy ourselves in order for the ego to merge with the soul. A unique provision in that Plan has therefore been implemented to ensure that humanity accomplishes that merger; and the Aquarian Agents™ referred to herein are the principal players.

Aquarian Agents™

Among the last revelations presented to me in 1976 was the work of the Oversouls and their Agents. The Agents, whose evolutionary tenure had advanced them into the Aquarian Age, agreed to return to the karmic system in order to facilitate its end. In so doing, they adopted, temporarily, certain of the conditions so intractably restricting the human collective.

These advanced souls who had evolved through all the karmic conditions still lingering on Earth came back to help dissolve those conditions by taking them on for a period of time. However, beyond their ego's consciousness, these souls had in their soul-force both the information and the inspiration to break out of these conditions. In so doing, they would leave an arc of information and inspiration in the collective consciousness for others, languishing in those conditions, to access that information and inspiration and thereby be able to break out of the karmic restrictions.

These Aquarian Agents™ would have chosen difficult childhoods, marriages, career challenges, values crises. They would be so advanced and gifted at the soul level — yet, restricted from utilizing and unleashing those gifts due to the limiting circumstances they had agreed to adopt and, ultimately, transform. At some level of their consciousness they would know that their life did not fully depict their qualities, their potential. Yet, each day they would experience their life in the typical pain of the human condition.

Eventually, however, the universe would convey to them, "It is now over. Your work at this level of service is complete. You will now be allocated the universal energies to express your gifts, your power, your purpose and your potential."

At that point, the Agent's life on Earth would begin to change. That individual's term in the karmic conditions would be over. Love, success, acceptance, prosperity, health — whatever that Agent's limitations, they would begin to be replaced with the qualities and opportunities befitting that great soul.

Oversouls

To make such sacrificial tours of duty possible, the universal consciousness created a unique complement to the Aquarian Agents'™ work: a one-time phenomenon referred to as Oversouls.

Their task is to register the qualities essential to inspiring the Aquarian Agents'™ work. Those qualities include truth, love, the right use of power, integrity, responsibility, accountability, courage, generosity, trust, equity, balance — and unwavering devotion to the principal Aquarian Age guideline: the greatest good for the greatest number.

To create an Oversoul, the universal consciousness momentarily suspended the evolution of certain of the souls that had registered significantly in the collective consciousness: Lincoln, Freud, Joan of Arc, Tchaikovsky, Moses, Shakespeare, Pasteur, Samson, etc. The soul force of these and a number of other inspiring individuals were then aggregated together to form a new type of soul force, the Oversouls. Their assignment is to serve one lifetime in that form. Then, the individual souls continue their evolution; and humanity would have been served in the meantime by the registering of significant power and greatness in the collective consciousness.

In essence, the Oversoul/Agent combination is the instrument the universal consciousness created to insure that humanity survives the challenges of passing into the 21st century. In Aquarian Numerology™, the number Two represents "understanding what you are to do." In the year 2000, each of the zeros represents the Godforce interacting with each of the three levels of human consciousness: the ego, subconscious and unconscious.

By the time that calendar event arrives, the ego and its entourage will have been put on notice. There will be no doubt in terms of what must be done to ensure the resources and information to preserve the future. The influence of the Oversouls will provide humanity with the qualities necessary to face the issues at hand. The work of the Agents will ensure that among the seemingly-impossible human conditions — anger, violence, corruption, incompetence, health care, fiscal imbalance, terrorism, infidelity to truth — those which can be transformed will have that process underway.

Conclusion

These are surely the times that try our souls. They bring forth the best from our souls, as well. And more than ever before, these times call out for the power and truth of our Being.

There is no greater purpose, no greater challenge, than to reclaim and manifest the divine right of our potential. It is bequeathed by the universe, administered by the soul, and urgently needed on this planet we call home.

Let us therefore call forth and reclaim the Authentic Self, unleashing at once, in all space and time, the truth of who we are, what we know and what we are here to do.

So Be it.

RECLAIMING THE AUTHENTIC SELF

Introduction

 As many persons of higher consciousness have experienced, it is often a struggle for our unique, gifted, sensitive self to find value and acceptance in the mundane world. Many times we have not been financially rewarded, or we felt the need to compromise in order to be so. In other ways we have not been able to attract the quality and quantity of love we need. Our insights and creativity have gone unnoticed or unfulfilled. And for many, patterns based on family-instilled insecurities restrict our purpose, power and potential.

At the same time, the world around us cries out for these gifts, these qualities, these demonstrations of love, courage, commitment and willingness to contribute to change. Indeed, it is an immense challenge not to give up, not to give in, but to hold out for a time when who we are and what we know enable us to do what we came here to do.

For some, that time is now. The call has gone out. The resources have been assembled to assist us in further awakening our purpose, unleashing our potential, and expressing our fullest capacity to Be, without consequences.

Finally! we say. And yet, when we look out onto the world — when we look at the anger, the imbalances, the misuse of resources, power and wealth — we might still reasonably wonder, How can I fit in? If I truly release from within me all that I know, all that I see, all that I am, how can I possibly find acceptance and fulfillment in the midst of that which is so unlike me?

In fact, given that many of us have tried, countless times, and found the incompatibilities too great, how are we to understand that this time it will be different? How are we to summon the courage and risk the disappointment? And why?

Why? Because at this point of crisis on this planet, the universe is finally releasing the energies to support us, and to create safe passage as we move through the structures that are in place. It is therefore time for us to act on what we see and what we know, and to challenge the power, the values, the economics, the governing bodies, the deceptions and the manipulations of truth.

All along it was divinely intended that we be different because we are here to make a difference. And to do that, we must reclaim from within ourselves the authentic, powerful, gifted self that, of necessity, adapted and edited itself in order to fit in. Now, however, we must come forth with those qualities we suppressed because they are essential to stewarding humanity's entry into the 21st century and the next, unprecedented, quantum evolution of consciousness.

Being Without Consequences

Reclaiming the Authentic Self provides the principles, guidelines and support for unleashing those qualities essential to humanity's next rite of passage into the realms of higher consciousness. At the individual level, the program assists in merging your ego and soul with the universal truth of your purpose and potential. In that process, the Authentic Self can be reclaimed in accordance with the key phrase of this program: Being, Without Consequences.

This experience is possible not only because humanity is now participating in the end of the karmic system. There are also energies and information being allocated to humanity's collective consciousness now that enable the human ego to connect with truth and Being unlike any preceding period in consciousness evolution.

Reclaiming the Authentic Self accesses those energies and principles for Being, without consequences. It helps you dissolve, through soul-directed change, the patterns that restrict the fullest expression of your unique, creative gifts. In so doing, the program enables you to connect with the universal energies now showering onto this planet to ensure that the purpose and gifts dedicated to you be fully engaged.

In this program, your courage will be tapped as you are shown how to cease adapting, and allow the universe to provide the environment for the expression of your fully powerful, purposeful Authentic Self.

The Ego and the Soul

The two most active levels of consciousness engaged in this program are the ego and the soul. For purposes of this program, the ego is the leading level of human consciousness. It is the consciousness that learns through experiences and evolves through its relationship with truth. The soul is the level of consciousness that oversees simultaneously the evolution of all three levels of consciousness assigned to humanity: ego, subconscious and unconscious. As the fourth dimension of consciousness, the soul is humanity's direct vibrational link to the universal consciousness, the creator consciousness that frequently is referred to as God. Accordingly, the soul is humanity's source of truth, which the soul communicates through intuition.

The other two levels of human consciousness, subconscious and unconscious, are also a part of this program. In their own relationship to truth, the subconscious stores truth and the unconscious blocks it. Patterns the ego has adopted at these two levels of consciousness will be challenged in this program so that their energies can be transformed into the power of authenticity: the truth of who you are, what you know, and what you are here to do.

How To Experience Reclaiming the Authentic Self

In the section immediately following, you will find the seven week program. It is comprised of 22 sets of guidelines: the Overview and 21 daily materials. It is recommended that you read the daily materials three mornings a week: Monday, Wednesday and Friday. Or, you can set aside an entire week to reflect on each set of guidelines.

The Materials

Depending on your reading style, absorbing the guidelines may require up to thirty minutes per reading — sometimes much less. A few of the days suggest a writing exercise, a ritual, or some other activity in addition to reading. Certain guidelines also refer you to supplementary reading and exercises contained in the section following the program guidelines. In most instances, one hour three times per week will enable you to fully participate in this program.

As you will notice, many of the guidelines refer to aspects of yourself you are to contemplate "today." If you read the guidelines three times per week, each day's guidelines apply for two days. If you read one set of guidelines per week, whatever is the focus for "today" will be with you for the week.

Additional Suggestions

The program is not just a one-time experience. You can repeat it many times. Each set of guidelines is like a matrix: a different set of insights into each set of guidelines will be activated each time you commence the program. Waiting at least three months before repeating it is recommended. However, this program is soul-directed. It knows how to find its way into your life at just the right time, and your soul will let you know when it is ready to work with you through the principles of this program.

It is ideal, but not necessary, for at least three persons to experience the program at the same time, reading the materials on the same days, sharing and discussing their experiences. The reason is that this program draws from a very powerful collective consciousness. It has been taught in groups of 15 - 20 for more than 15 years. As a result of the strong collective consciousness already created, your own experience of these materials will be enhanced.

While experiencing these materials, it is also helpful to remember the variety of forms that transformational healing may embody in a program such as this one. Be sure to eat well, exercise regularly, breathe deeply and, above all, do not try to hurry the program. Let it work with your own unique schedule and needs.

Have Fun!

If you choose, you may journal or record your dreams as the program progresses. You may want to write a "Letter of Readiness" in the beginning, signifying the changes you are ready to make. If so, seal the letter and read it one month after finishing the program. The period three to four weeks after the program is often quite dynamic due to the settling of certain energies which the program dynamics either activate or reorganize.

It is also important to have fun while you are participating in this program. Some moments of it will be a bit intense. They will purposefully cause you to look at some aspects of your life that are somewhat sobering. In the midst of it, however, break up your usual routine with some fun. Use your spontaneous creativity to stimulate your enjoyment of life even as you focus on aspects you do not enjoy and earnestly want to change.

Especially if there is something you have been thinking about doing . . . do it now. This program urges you to break up patterns so that their energy can be reallocated to activate your potential. Denying yourself pleasure, fun and enjoyment is a perfect pattern to challenge.

Let Us Hear From You

Because your comments would be greatly appreciated, please write and share with us your experience. There are many gifted, courageous souls like you who have created the path for this program. Thanks to them, this information is available. And thanks also to you for being a part of this journey for Reclaiming Your Authentic Self.

RECLAIMING THE AUTHENTIC SELF

A Dynamic Seven Week

Program

OVERVIEW

Guidelines:

The power to Be is within.

The Challenge of Truth

Being is the ego's fullest expression of its truth and potential at any given moment. Truth is the information that comes to the ego through the soul from the creator consciousness referred to as God. It is the mechanism by which human consciousness evolves, and it contains the guidance and courage that enable the ego to Be. The source of energy to Be, as well as the inspiration and information for how to manifest Being on Earth, have been placed within each divinely created individual.

For humanity as a whole, the challenges of Being are formidable, particularly because the human ego often ignores, denies, or manipulates the truth — its source of guidance for Being. Even for highly intuitive persons, the early life challenges and consequences of Being were often unbearable, because their environment neither acknowledged the truth of who they were nor supported the truth of what they were here to do. As a result, the unique, sensitive, gifted aspects of those individuals were often forfeited or suppressed in an effort to fit in, be acceptable, and find love within those circumstances.

As one of those persons whose assignment it is to bring the power of Being into full expression, with no precedent or model for doing so, you would have experienced some degree of pain in adapting to early life circumstances. Those circumstances were undoubtedly inadequate, perhaps even contrary to the truth of who you are, what you know, what you feel, what you need, and what you are here to do. At the same time, however, the strength and courage you summoned from within to adapt, and thereby withstand those circumstances, can now support the emergence of the authentic self.

In certain earlier situations, your authentic self may have been unable to challenge or to withstand the value systems and circumstances it regularly faced. So it compromised, adapting the truth of its being to the limitations of the situations into which it had been placed. Adapting under those circumstances was the highest choice because it was the only choice. That environment was incapable of valuing or supporting your creative, sensitive, loving, authentic self.

The Message of Truth

But the toll has been great — for you, for all the other extraordinary individuals who have likewise compromised, and for the planet as well. Withholding the power of those creative, sensitive, loving qualities, and the collective potential thereby suppressed, has left room on the planet for immense buildups to the contrary. Thus, an urgent message is now going out to individuals who have pursued the path of restricted Being: No more. No longer. The time has come to release your knowing, powerful self.

The universe has allocated the guidelines and the resources necessary to ensure the security and success of Being. Those guidelines come through the soul; they awaken the resources within, and together, the guidelines and resources manifest in a manner that dissolves the old and creates a new value for, and an outcome to, Being.

The courage to Be requires immense trust of this universe. Therefore, to mobilize that courage, the universe asks only that the self know the truth. What is the truth of who I am? Not what I have been, or tried to be, or acted like or said . . . but what is the truth of that which is within me? That which *is* me? That which I Am?

Even though that which you are has been suppressed, even though it has been manipulated at times, even though it has compromised and misled itself, and others, in an effort to find and figure out a way to fit in, to be rewarded and successful and secure and fulfilled; even though at times it has done whatever it needed to do to get through the moment or the crisis or the relationship or job task . . . even so, because that authentic self once was created, it always will be.

Despite the ego's need or effort to edit it, manipulate it, deny it or destroy bits of it at times, the authentic self remains in the essence, if not in the expression, of the individual.

The Truth of the Authentic Self

Because the authentic, divinely created self always has been, and will always be, deep within, for the remainder of this lifetime, it is important for the ego self to realize that despite its efforts, fears and fantasies to the contrary, the ego has not materially affected the authentic self. Maybe it denied that self or abused its integrity or misused its creative power and potential. But that authentic, gifted self was created by the universe to serve this planet. And no ego, even though also created by this universe, will be given the power or potential to destroy it.

The ego can deny the authentic self because denial is one of the ego's weapons against truth. But even if it denies the authentic self, the ego cannot destroy it. The authentic self is the truth of the universe's creation — and every moment, the universe creates the potential for that authentic self to say or feel or know in accordance with its purpose. If, in relation to one of those moments, the ego fears the consequences of such truth and edits or amends itself accordingly, then the pain and angst of that choice pierces the ego, but not the authentic self.

For too long, too many persons on this planet have lived in fear of the consequences of the truth. As a result, without truth to intercede, a convergence of threatening conditions now challenges the human collective. By reclaiming the power of truth, humanity will experience the courage and creativity to reverse these conditions. To do otherwise puts our natural resources, economic security, and emotional and physical well-being at risk.

The human ego is therefore being challenged to know and express the truth; to cease its inclination to deny, fear, manipulate or withhold the truth; and to release from within, as a result, the powerful and essential authentic self.

DAY NUMBER ONE

Guidelines:

The willingness to end; the courage to begin.

The exchange of the adaptive self for the authentic self creates a vortex of simultaneous, oppositely flowing energies. To accomplish that exchange, the truth of how the adaptive self has functioned must be fully identified. That self has, after all, served a purpose. It was created so that the alienated, authentic self could survive. Thus, before the adaptive self can be released, its role and purpose must be acknowledged in a deep, probing manner. To do so involves scanning the repertoire of that self that has functioned for years, verifying that each nuance of personality, needs, emotions and capacities has served its potential, reached the fulfillment of its purpose, and is thereby prepared to yield to the emergence of the authentic self.

Truth is that probing energy, identifying compassionately and powerfully each aspect of the adaptive self that is ready to be replaced. The conscious ego of that self knows the truth. Truth is a constant. Furthermore, just because the adaptive self positioned itself outside the truth does not mean it obscured the truth from others. When the adaptive self hid its true self in an effort to be liked or to get a better job, such an effort appeared to succeed only in the presence of others who operated the same way: knowing the truth but pretending otherwise. Hiding the truth never really changed the truth, nor did it alter the inevitable outcome that truth was designated to produce. Hiding or manipulating truth only postpones the outcome which the universe has set in motion by way of truth.

Releasing the Adaptive

This type of adaptive approach, to varying degrees, has been a lifestyle for persons of higher consciousness because they concluded early in their experience that there was not a value for their way of Being. Thus, the first focus of the Authentic Self program is to convey to the adaptive ego that its efforts, for so long essential to its very survival, are no longer necessary. In fact, they will no longer succeed . . . because the universe is now releasing onto this planet the energies to support the revival of truth, and the truth of the authentic self can now safely and purposefully be revealed. The purpose of the first phase of this program is, therefore, to create the guidelines and support for you to acknowledge the truth, the toll, and the release of the adaptive self.

Know, therefore, that whatever you have done, however you have done it, and whatever explanations you have applied in the process . . . it was, at all times, the best you could do. There was neither adequate love nor truth available for your ego to have done anything else. That is the crisis this planet faces at this time. To assist in reversing that, you are being shown how to access the love and truth essential to creating a sustainable quality of life. And in the evolution of human consciousness, truth is the energy by which the ego evolves . . . and humanity's direct source of truth is the soul. As humanity positions itself for entry into Aquarian Age consciousness, it must calibrate the ego to follow soul guidance. That is the essence of the next, quantum, step in consciousness: for the ego to receive and register direct input from the universal consciousness through the soul.

The Soul's Guidance

The universal consciousness which has created the answers to save the future must both manifest the necessary answers and direct the necessary resources onto the Earth plane through the ego. Ego is the highest level of human consciousness assigned to the Earth plane, and it is through that consciousness that the information, resources and changes will be derived. Accordingly, to receive the guidance and access the resources, the ego must be following the truth — the soul's communication. Thus, the ego's need to adapt the truth of its authentic self must be transformed so that the truth of its purpose and potential can be revealed. Once it is revealed through the soul, that purpose and potential must be manifested through the ego. And the first principle of manifestation for the human consciousness is to Be. On this first day of this program you are therefore invited to spend the next few moments contemplating Being — envisioning what your life and contributions to the planet could be if you had all the resources to express your fullest potential.

Know that the universal consciousness which created that potential has also created the resources for it to manifest. Adapting up to this point has been necessary, but as you surely know, it has never brought you close to the outcomes you envisioned, or deserved. Now, however, if you are prepared to be led to Be otherwise, the universe will be able to create and manifest for you, and through you, the outcomes that have always been within your potential. The guidance for unleashing that potential comes through the soul, which challenges the ego to trust the truth and be willing constantly to express without editing or adapting who you are, what you know, what you feel, what you need, and what you are here to do.

Your soul knows that you long ago lost the constant contact with your essence and authenticity. Your soul has watched compassionately as your ego regularly assembled and packaged itself in variations of authenticity. Your soul knows that, as a result, you do not know how to Be to your fullest potential. But because your soul does know how to guide you into that expression, the cooperation it needs at the ego level is simple: know the truth and be willing to follow the soul's guidance in expressing it.

Using the Ego's Will

Following the soul's guidance means challenging the ego's automatic, adaptive patterns. It means using the ego's will to acknowledge those patterns at their onset, to refuse to employ them, and then to await the soul's guidance for how to replace the patterns with authenticity. This certainly takes courage on the part of the ego, because its memory is that its true self — which is sensitive, creative, unique, loving and powerful — is not acceptable, is not lovable, is not compatible with an insensitive, unloving, inauthentic world. Thus, the ego fears that to reconnect with that self and offer it to the world now will be as painful as whatever originally caused the ego to abandon that self and assemble one not so vulnerable.

The ego might even question how, in a world that has gotten even more insensitive and inauthentic, can the essence of Who I Am truly find recognition? There are two answers. One is that the universal consciousness overseeing the evolution of life on Planet Earth has now unleashed energies from the Aquarian Age to reverse many of the conditions threatening the planet's future. Those are the same conditions that have threatened your own essence (your own authenticity) and they are in varying stages of disintegration and transformation. The other answer relates more specifically to the ego's role and security in the reversal of those conditions: the ego itself, as humanity's leading level of consciousness, is being transformed so that it can steward the energies destined to accomplish such reversal. Thus, the ego's access to truth is being enhanced, and the outcome of its expression of truth is being powerfully rewarded.

However, conditions created by the ego in disregard of the truth cannot be reversed by an adaptive ego similarly engaged. Therefore, the necessary transformation of adaptive to authentic in this program is accomplished in a vortex wherein, immediately following the ego's acknowledgment of the adaptive patterns it has adopted, the energy of those patterns dissolves and is allocated to commence the expression of the authentic self.

Within the vortex created to accommodate this exchange of conditions, truth releases the former condition and simultaneously creates the new. The ego's willingness not to engage in the familiar, adaptive behavior leaves space for the soul to add the new behavior: the essence of the authentic self, reclaimed. In the context of this program you are asked to experience the joy and relief of releasing the old — to trust the universe and its agent of evolution, the soul — and to commit to the highest expression of your courage and integrity in this program for reclaiming your own authentic self.

DAY NUMBER TWO

Guidelines:

A void waits to be filled.

In the vortex of consciousness transformation, where energies opposite from one another (*i.e.*, the adaptive vs. the authentic) flow simultaneously, a sacred moment occurs when the two meet equally — each with the same power and momentum as the other, neither with sufficient dominion to prevail.

In this space, a new expression of consciousness is created. All the energy from one direction is a reflection of that which has been (the adaptive). The other energy is pure potential (the authentic); it never has been expressed, even though it has always *been*. A particular interaction is necessary for that authentic potential to be manifested. The energy to aid it must be unleashed, which means that that energy must have fully served its purpose in one form (adaptive) and be ready to take another form (authentic).

The intangible potential within an individual (the authentic) is released only when a mass of energy opposite from that potential (the adaptive) is prepared to give itself entirely, by transformation, to become the registrar of that (authentic) potential. Otherwise the potential would remain in its unrefined, unmanifested and unmanifestable state.

It is this transaction in the contract for higher consciousness that explains why a gifted, creative individual might languish in conditions totally unlike and noncomplementary to that person's potential. Indeed, because that potential is etched, although not manifested, in that person's essence, it is often confounding to that person to have both that unrealized potential, as well as the reality of day to day circumstances, contained in that person's consciousness: a "who I am" versus "what I am doing" juxtaposition.

The Vortex

In this program, a vortex of consciousness exchange is created to address this condition. The energy in this vortex that *has* served its purpose (the adaptive) has only the culminating moment of that purpose remaining — then that energy will be emptied. That which has been will give life to that which is to be. Thus, in that single moment of emptying — combined with the potential that is awakened by that state of emptiness — an awesome, unprecedented possibility is produced. The void creates the space for the new to occupy; and until the void is created — until the energies of the adaptive self vacate and co-create the void — the impulse for the new cannot ignite.

In other words, in this quantum consciousness experience, that which *has been* does not simply continue its gradual, orderly, linear, change-based evolution. It ceases. The reason is that, in order to express fully its Being, the authentic is not, and cannot be, simply less adaptive. It Is, and it must Be. Fully. Completely. Only. Otherwise it is not at all. Therefore, the energy of the adaptive self, created by the ego, must vacate to allow the authentic, created by the soul.

In that quantum moment within the vortex, that which ceases to be is sparked by awareness, into nothingness, with the truth of its potential, its value,

Reclaiming the Authentic Self

and its purpose having been revealed. That truth which the ego allows pours so deeply into itself that all that is incompatible with truth dissolves. This transaction simultaneously allows the truth to create, in its place and with its vacated energy, the presence and potential of the authentic. All that it ever can be is thereby manifested in that vortex of consciousness.

When that moment of quantum consciousness is manifested, it revisits the universal moment when the individual consciousness was created by the divine; when the purpose and potential for that individual first were formed; and when the energy of the individual, Being, was first conceived. At that moment of first creation — when the universe allocated the energy as well as the consciousness for the individual to manifest — all that the individual was to be in that given lifetime was registered in a macro-conscious moment.

For the ego consciousness now to reconnect with the energies of that moment is a quantum consciousness experience. The ego consciousness, filled with the energy of that which it has been, is exchanged for that which it has the potential to become.

And, once the connection is made, the ego has that vibrational connector as a constant reference point. It is, in essence, the truth of the individual's path and the resources divinely allocated thereupon.

How To Consciously Participate

Because this program gathers unto it both the collective vibration as well as the individual vortex vibration for this exchange — from whom one has been, into whom one has the potential to become — you are asked to review on this day what this exchange means in each aspect of your life.

For example, the energies of the vortex are a "release and Be" combination: the ego lets go of the old, the universe creates the new. If in your own circumstances you are inclined to hold onto some one or some thing because you are convinced they are essential to your life, then be assured that such holding on is neither necessary nor productive. The universe knows what you need. It knows what you have. It designed, created and allocated to you everything that you have.

If the universe truly wants you to have something, your releasing it will not cause you to lose it. The universe will simply reward your courage and willingness to release by adding a bit more meaning or purpose or service or consciousness to that which you have courageously been willing to release. In other words, your being willing to release something may allow it to remain with you in a state of higher consciousness. If, however, the universe has created something even better and wants to support you accordingly, it is important that you not resist. Release in your consciousness *all* that is old so that *all* that is newly directed toward you, in consciousness or tangible form, can be manifested.

Releasing Into The Void

The Void is the objective. The interchange of the two dynamics in the vortex creates an extraordinary space for awareness, courage, power, inspiration . . . whatever is required to assist the manifestation of the authentic self. In the dynamics of this very powerful program, the ego will be led to release only with awareness. Only the truth will be used to jar loose anything within or around the adaptive self that has served its purpose and now needs to be replaced.

For this day's exercise in consciousness transformation, value the void. Above all, do not fear it The void creates the space for that which you need to come to you. Welcome it. Trust it. Release yourself, for this one day, from all expectations or certainties about who you are, or are not; what you do, or do not, need; what is adaptive; what is authentic; what is unproductive; what is not. Suspend your ego consciousness and allow the universe to bring you to the consciousness of your potential as the universe created it, not as your ego has edited or forfeited it. Allow the spark of your willingness to catalyze the energy of that potential — because once it is manifested in your consciousness, the energy for it to Be, to unfold, and to replace the adaptive with the authentic is underway.

DAY NUMBER THREE

Guidelines:

Knowing the truth of who I am.

The truth of who you are, deep inside, in your divinely created potential, is undoubtedly different from the you that has expressed itself throughout the years of this lifetime. It is important to know the truth of that adaptive self, however, even though the emphasis of this program is the authentic self. One reason to know both is to consciously steward the exchange of one for the manifestation of the other.

On this day you are asked to examine the qualities within you: qualities that denote your potential for Being. You are also asked this day to acknowledge what has kept you from expressing that divinely created potential, and kept you from Being that authentic, powerful, creative, liberated self. Look, therefore, at those aspects of yourself that do not manifest in accordance with the standards the universe has given you . . . because those standards are the framework into which your potential is to be manifested. And until you create an adequate framework, that powerful potential cannot be unleashed. (To reflect more specifically on your standards and qualities, refer to "Examining My Relationship with Myself," on page 102.)

Qualities create that framework. Consider, therefore, the quality of your own accountability. Do you acknowledge unwaveringly when you have not kept your word, or followed through, or forgotten, or completed something with a lesser standard than you committed? In such instances, do you admit the truth? Or do you try to explain, give reasons, or cite circumstances that make your ego look "better?" If any of these options or tendencies are in your ego's repertoire, you can expect your soul to start stripping them away immediately, assisting you in replacing them with a higher capacity to be accountable. And truthful.

Ego Tests

This type of soul-directed examination is directed toward and through the ego that is willing to express itself truthfully — not inclined to edit, manipulate or control the directives for Being, which come through truth. This potential for Being is derived from the higher planes, and directed onto Earth to dissolve and replace the ego's limited potential. Any ego volunteering for this exchange is prepared because its very creation and evolution have anticipated this moment. As a result, the ego is not given time to think this over; or to try it out to see if it works or if it feels better. Neither is the ego given the opportunity to test whether it can still be liked or financially successful if it follows this higher standard of expression, reserving the right to commit to this standard only after trying it out.

The ego has been waiting desperately for this moment. It will not be allowed to manipulate the moment when it arrives.

The adaptive ego has known deep inside that it had potential it would never fulfill, given the choices and patterns it perpetuated. That ego has asked regularly for assistance in releasing its potential. Thus, when the truth of how to release that potential comes into its awareness, the ego must follow that truth.

Truth *is* the energy comprising that potential. It is also the energy for releasing it. Because of the way the ego has historically functioned, it *will* be given a window of time to adjust to the vibration of such guidance. But the ego must commence its willingness to "express the truth of who I am" now. Then, as the ego follows one directive for how to Be, and discovers that it works, another, barely more challenging directive will be given. It too will work. And since these initial directives are allocated only as the ego's resources and readiness allow, the ego does not fail. In addition, these soul directives are spread throughout the ego's daily routines. This enables the ego to experience the qualitative difference these applied directives create within its regular (adaptive) routine.

Qualities of Authenticity

In this manner the ego's accountability is refined even further. The ego is accountable not only for what it says and does; it is now accountable for the truth and awareness revealed to it as its adaptive self is dismantled. In that process the ego is given the guidance for directing the expression of its authentic self. Accountability is an asset essential to authenticity. Other qualities become equally essential assets: integrity, courage, honesty, compassion, discrimination, balance and order, for example. When these qualities are in place, they reflect and reveal the truth. When they are absent, or inconsistent, so is the truth within and around an individual. To the authentic self, these qualities are security. Any thing or any one that cannot withstand or complement them is never a loss — only an opportunity to renew within the love and respect one feels in relationship with truth, and the courage one feels in expressing that truth.

Accordingly, integrity is the human expression of one's relationship with truth; and, because truth is constant, so is integrity. It is unequivocating. There is no room for considering even a minor deviation from the truth, including the truth of not being accountable. If you forgot to call someone, for example, you were not accountable because you did not keep your word. Your integrity is still intact, however, when you say the truth: I forgot. To subscribe to the "little white lie" syndrome, however, is deadly to the authentic self. There are no white lies. There is truth . . . and everything else.

Each individual is held accountable for the highest truth accessible within one's consciousness at any given moment. It is not the ego's task to select or reject or manipulate truth. The ego's principal *challenge* is to *know* the truth; its principal *assignment* is to *say* the truth. Its greatest jeopardy is to fear the truth. And given that the human ego has actually reached the point of fearing the truth, to restore the ego's relationship with truth will inevitably require another essential quality: courage. Courage is the quality that bypasses the ego's doubts, fears, manipulations and infidelity to truth. It is a supporting mechanism that automatically engages to assist the ego in saying what is true and doing what is right.

Courage does, therefore, enable humanity to be honest. In general, honesty is telling the truth. In money matters, it means returning or refusing whatever is not divinely, ethically right, including reporting all income and paying appropriate taxes. The universe will give us all the money we need in order to be honest. In addition, because accountability includes abiding by laws, so long as the human collective is bound by laws such as taxation, it is not the task of any individual ego to determine the fairness of such a law, or that individual's exemption therefrom. Inequitable, corrupt, self-serving systems will collapse on their own merits as the redistribution of power and resources proceeds. Individuals will be much better served in the meantime spending their energies to be honest — not trying to outwit or outmaneuver massive systems that will only feed on and consume their energies, resources and misdirected power.

Whatever laws the universe has placed in the hands of humanity, the universe will hold humanity accountable for them until those laws have served their purpose. Until then, the human ego has much to learn from obeying those laws, whether the learning comes from the courage to honor them or the temptation — or consequences — relative to breaking them.

On this day of knowing the truth of who you are, review your own qualities and consistencies in relation to the above. If you have the capacity to express these qualities more powerfully, allow your soul to guide you in doing so. It is in keeping with reclaiming the authentic self.

DAY NUMBER FOUR

Guidelines:

As the familiar is restricted, the authentic is formed.

Change is underway. Certain systems within the psyche are on alert.

Subconscious patterns that have served the ego for years cling to the reality that established them, because without that reality — the *I can't, I should, it's my fault, I feel guilty, I'm not good enough* routines — those patterns are history. Irrespective of the truth, within those patterns lies a belief that they are necessary. The ego believes that without those patterns as a functional, protective tool, it will fail. It will be unloved. It will not succeed. It will succumb to the fears and dreads it managed to escape and cover up with the subconscious patterns.

Examples of those patterns that have served the ego include acting in a manner that hopefully will attract love (but does not); buying and accumulating and surrounding self with demonstrations of success (which only disguise emptiness); denying fear, anger, sadness and doubts, thereby preventing love (which is the real need) by attracting others with the same emotional inadequacies and insecurities that occasioned the patterns originally.

Truth And Love

These patterns only, and inevitably, produce consequences because they are contrary to the truth. The primary consequence, alienation from truth, produces alienation from love . . . because love is humanity's emotional reward for its courage to express the truth. And the quality and quantity of truth in one's life determines the quality and quantity of love. Furthermore, individuals attract the quality and quantity of truth they live. Therefore, because they attract love according to the quality and quantity of love within, *needing* love does not attract love. Needing love attracts others who need love. Having love within, to give, attracts others who have love within, to give. In fact, the catalytic dynamic of love interacting with love is what creates *more* love in a relationship. But having an inadequate amount of love within, which creates a *need* for love, attracts others in the same condition . . . because someone who has love within will be attracted to love, not to need.

Needs do have compelling dynamics. The need for love may bring people together, but that need can be so intense it gets confused with the intensity of love. Whereas love is the creative emotion, ensuring that the more love there is, the more love will be created, the opposite is true of needs. The greater the need for love, the less capacity to give love. As a result, the supply of love initially available in an individual or a relationship is drained soon. That supply is inevitably inadequate to meet the need for love that has built up for decades, thus the relationship inevitably meets its limitations. When the reality of the love being inadequate to meet the needs finally settles in, the automatic emotional response is anger.

Truth And Anger

In the arena of authenticity, the topic of emotional integrity, specifically as it relates to anger, must be addressed. Ideally this planet eventually will evolve its relationship with truth sufficiently to create an adequate amount of love. In the next Age of Aquarius, humanity will have reached that evolutionary point.

Emotional Integrity

At this time, however, truth and love are not so abundant . . . and anger is the result. Being angry is not inconsistent with being spiritual or loving. Anger is a God-given emotion and it has a purpose. Until humanity's relationship with truth evolves sufficiently to create more love on this planet, anger is here to challenge love to expand. Denying anger, suppressing it, enabling it to accumulate into rage . . . these are all issues of emotional integrity. If the truth is "I am angry," but the anger is manipulated by denial or suppression, then the individual was not honest, not accountable, and that disruptive emotional energy turned destructive. (The additional article, "Emotional Integrity," on page 134 will add insights to this topic.)

Love is humanity's automatic emotional response when its needs are met. Anger is humanity's automatic emotional response when its needs are *not* met. However, since the purpose of anger is to create change, the change anger elicits is in relation to love. Anger challenges love to expand. The hidden message behind anger is "I need to feel more love." Thus, anger stirs up the conditions in place and, with its purposefully intense, disturbing energy, anger challenges the current availability of love to expand — to reach its fullest potential.

The individual's experience of inadequate love in early life causes subconscious patterns to form. While in some instances the love was there but the individual could not experience it, often the individual experienced an inadequate supply of love because the anger in early life situations built up to become rage. Unlike anger, which has the capacity to *create* change, rage is destructive. It destroys the conditions that produce love. Anger is more intense than love, but love is more enduring. Thus, anger and love coexist. A person who is angry is not unloving. Anger is simply the dominant emotion for a brief period of time. Once it is expressed, however, and serves its purpose (to challenge love to expand), the anger goes away . . . and the love, which is constant and enduring, is again dominant.

For the masses, the purpose of life on Earth is to learn about love. For persons of higher consciousness, their purpose is to reverse patterns restricting love, such as suppressing or denying anger, and to register a new way of experiencing and expressing love. That reversal begins by understanding the purpose of those restrictive patterns — understanding that the patterns were voluntarily adopted by evolved, dedicated souls who chose parents and early life situations similar to those that are severely affecting this planet. The conditions these souls took on were extremely inadequate — painfully incapable of responding to, valuing, trusting and unconditionally loving their unique, gifted, sensitive selves.

These souls who took on this task of reversing conditions on Earth have come into this lifetime with a reservoir of love within, and a significant connection with universal love. Prior to this lifetime, these souls had been experiencing the love vibration of the next evolutionary age — Aquarius — wherein humanity no longer is encumbered with a subconscious and unconscious requiring lessons and consequences. The love in that Age is constant. To "make" love is impossible anyway; and in the Aquarian Age it is unthinkable. Love simply *is* in the Aquarian Age. And with no lower consciousness obstructing, denying or manipulating truth, love and truth are constants in that Age.

For persons of higher consciousness brought back from the Aquarian Age to the Earth plane to express here that love/truth connection, their *purpose* is related to that assignment: they are here to experience and express a quality of love that, until now, was not available to humanity, principally because the human ego was insufficiently evolved to manifest a constant relationship with truth — and thereby, with love.

But at this point of crisis in consciousness, the effects of the ego unconnected with truth and love are dire. Greed, corruption, abuse, misinformation, exploitation, violence . . . the consequences are numerous and increasing. In addition, resources on the planet are being ravaged and consumed in an effort to avoid the realities accumulating. Thus, there is a convergence of conditions of unprecedented proportions, the dismantling of which each one of us can be a part, by contributing to creating the opposite of that which has allowed these conditions: untruth and unlove. On this day of this program, reflect on your own relationship with truth and, therefore, love.

DAY NUMBER FIVE

Guidelines:

With insights in place, meaningful changes begin.

The purpose of life on Earth is to teach us about love. The purpose of lessons related to love is to teach the consequences of untruth, which leads to unlove. Whether you are firmly planted in the venue of life that reflects your purpose, making progress toward it, or orbiting without a clue, you can know that connecting more strongly to your purpose requires examining and changing — perhaps drastically, perhaps only slightly — your relationship with love/truth.

Starting first with yourself, and your self-love, know that self-love increases when we do what is good for ourselves — what our intuition/soul guidance leads us to do, or change. Likewise, self-love is sabotaged or diminished when we do those things that are counterproductive, and when we deny or defer communication from the soul.

Soul Love

The soul is humanity's direct vibrational link to the creative universal consciousness that communicates and connects with us through truth. The soul is humanity's only constant source of unconditional love. In addition, based on the quality and quantity of love within us — which must come from our soul and our self — we attract (or do not attract) love from others. Humanity's only experience of love, however, is within . Rather than loving another, it would be more accurate to say, "I love the feelings inside me that your presence in my life creates." The love is inside. Depending on another person's love vibration, the energy of their vibration connects with the energy field of our own vibration and we feel a response inside. That internal response is based on the other person's capacity to activate the love that is within.

On this day for examining changes to make in relation to self-love, set aside some minutes of quiet reflective time and listen to your soul. Allow it to review for you the guidance it has offered regarding your relationship with love. Know that whatever you realize today is part of a greater message in relation to you and love, you and truth, you and purpose. Know also that your soul has within its consciousness and dominion all of the information and resources you will require in order to do what you came here to do. Your soul knows not only your purpose this lifetime, and each step you must take along the way; it also knows the purpose of each "mis-step" — each willful choice or denial, each hesitation, each doubt or fear. And because *its* purpose is to disburse resources as abundantly and immediately as possible, the soul vigilantly monitors every moment of your consciousness, looking for the tiniest opening to allocate those resources. They include love, insight, awareness, caution, reflection, and guidance for understanding the purpose of each moment.

Doing vs. Being

In today's exercise of soul communication, look carefully at your ego's will — its tendency for "doing." Even though soul-*guided* doing is part of being on

Earth, often when the ego is focused on doing, it is not in a receiving mode . . . and receiving soul guidance is essential. As the ego has discovered, there is lots to *do* on planet Earth. But doing, without purpose, is a way to avoid soul guidance. If the ego can assure itself it does not have "time" to follow the soul's directives then it can postpone those directives, and all the meaningful changes they can produce. In communing with your soul about love today, examine whether you have "time" for love, and for the other quality-of-life changes your soul is suggesting. "How do I tell the difference between soul guidance and ego?" is one of humanity's crucial questions. It often does not like the answer, however, because one strong indication of soul guidance is the ego's response: it often does not like what the soul is suggesting. When the ego employs doubt, which is its strongest weapon against truth, that is a clear example of the ego battling the soul.

Along those lines, the adaptive self may not like certain of the soul's directives for reclaiming the authentic self. Nevertheless, the soul is *the* source of creative energies for activating and reclaiming the authentic self. Thus, it is important for the ego to implement the "small" changes because they create the pathway for the rest.

In communing with the adaptive self, the soul will reflect on the choices that adaptive self has made, revealing to it that because the truth is always present, the truth of an outcome is always present at the onset of an experience. In the past, therefore, when the self made an unproductive choice, it had to have avoided some clue about the truth . . . because the truth is always present, even when egos are consumed in denying, misrepresenting or changing it. In this program, those truths will be revealed so those patterns can be transformed.

Truth Or Consequences

The ego's challenge is, stated simply, Truth *or* Consequences. When the ego denies the truth, the universe immediately allocates the unused energy of that truth to set up a series of lessons and experiences to lead the ego back to that truth. If it is a particularly difficult truth to acknowledge, that truth may be continuously presented and have its denied energies redistributed into lessons numerous times. If so, the result is patterns: similar situations that hook the ego into similar, yet slightly different situations with the same underlying theme . . . the same truth initially denied.

From the soul's perspective, because each of its communications to the ego is truth, each particle of its information is as important as any other. All soul communications are part of the matrix that establishes the ego's connection with truth and love. Thus, the ego that longs for revelations or reassurances about its purpose may be blocking that "larger" soul guidance because the channel for soul directions is clogged with "smaller" (according to the ego) pieces of information it has chosen to ignore: balancing the checkbook, rotating the tires, writing a thank-you letter, cleaning out the basement, eating out less and cooking at home more, etc.

Unbeknownst to the ego, in addition to being accountable, there are other valuable reasons for following soul guidance on mundane matters. The soul is prepared to sprinkle droplets of creative inspiration into the ego's consciousness while it is engaged in those mundane, accountable tasks. The soul even regularly nudges and reminds the ego to commence these tasks, so eager is the soul to bring these gifts and rewards to the struggling, unsuspecting ego. But because the ego does not have time to rotate the tires, a relationship the ego longs for is delayed — because that is how they will meet. Likewise with the checkbook: once it is balanced, a job promotion can be released.

In your own life, reclaim the connection with your soul today, acknowledging its guidance for self-love and the changes essential to expressing the authentic self. Start making the changes you know are good for you.

DAY NUMBER SIX

Guidelines:
Understanding the Purpose of My Authentic Self.

Like a butterfly emerging from a cocoon, the authentic self is being released from the karmic, consequence-based evolutionary plan. Whereas the butterfly has been encased in the cocoon, its beauty and potential not evident, the authentic self has likewise been encased in the protective shell of the adaptive self, with its beauty and potential hidden as well. The contrast between who it has been and who it is to become is equally awesome. The purpose of the caterpillar had always been for it to become a butterfly, and the purpose of the adaptive self was for it to become the authentic self. In this program, the measures for enabling that metamorphosis are underway: the adaptive self yielding, the authentic self building, the soul guiding, and the universal consciousness creating this extraordinary component of consciousness evolution.

The Dismantling

In the why, how and when aspects to this phenomenon, the overarching why is that the human condition, produced and directed by the human ego, has created far more, and far more complex, conditions on planet Earth than it has the resources to resolve. Therefore, a crisis in consciousness — an evolutionary breakthrough moment — is at hand. It occurs now because the Aquarian Age is approaching, its energies already showering onto the Earth's consciousness. It is an era of ego and soul merger with no subconscious and unconscious to distort or deny truth. Thus, whatever is currently in place on Earth as repositories of subconscious and unconscious energies, is being dismantled — targeted for transformation. The consciousness of those repositories is being penetrated by the truth, which thereby illuminates and eliminates anything constructed upon or around alternatives to the truth. Institutions, bureaucracies, governments, belief systems . . . any aggregate of energy that is self-serving, misusing power, withholding or denying or misrepresenting the truth . . . their energies will be dismantled. Those energies will be neutralized in the cosmos so that, when they return, they will be able to serve only the collective, not the individual ego.

As a person of higher consciousness, willing to honor soul guidance, you have been prepared to contribute to the creating of sustainable values as those neutralized energies now return to Earth. At the moment your soul received its assignment on Earth for this lifetime, it knew it was to work in a traditional manner (*i.e.*, evolving through the karmic system of lessons and consequences) for the first phase of this lifetime, watching over and stewarding the ego through the typical trials and tribulations of choices relative to truth. Your soul also knew that when the karmic system began to give way to the next Age and its principles for ego evolution, your ego would be tapped to create the consciousness for that transition.

The Call

That call, for the emergence of the authentic self, has now been made. Under the guidelines of that challenge, the information for the consciousness of transition from ego-based to soul-created expression on Earth is revealed. Through the soul, the information, inspiration, resources and principles for creating sustainable values and lifestyles are available. None of those is creatable by the ego, which has used its substantial creativity to serve itself. While that is typical of the ego — and while the universal consciousness created the abundance of both the Earth plane and the three-dimensional, material plane in sufficient quantity to serve the evolution of the ego in this consumption, destruction model — it is now time to reverse that.

The resources to make the world better, not the self greater, are assembled in the fourth dimension of soul stewardship. However, because the soul does not operate in the dimensions of human consciousness assigned to Earth, to ensure that those resources reach the Earth plane in the manner and for the purpose intended, the soul must work with and through the ego level of consciousness. As an Aquarian Agent™, your consciousness is being prepared for this role in the redistribution of information, inspiration, creativity, principles, resources, power, love and truth. All of these are contained in the band of consciousness encircling Earth. They are the energy to produce the transition that is underway.

When the human ego is in place, that transition is signaled by the adaptive self giving way to the authentic. In that process, wherein the adaptive self passes through a variety of segments in its transition out of the karmic system, one of the most significant is its learning the power of Being without consequences. That possibility is both contrary to the ego's experience and completely without precedent on the Earth plane. The collective consciousness amassed on the Earth plane is totally comprised of consequence-based information. As a result, not only is there no collective consciousness available to support the individual ego in its transition; there is instead a formidable collection of energy supporting the former. The ego is therefore being challenged to disregard and, with soul guidance, override the karmic conditioning and belief systems in order to allow the emerging of the authentic self.

The End Of Karma

This quantum transition to truth from consequences is possible because it is the next phase of the ego's evolution in accordance with the divine plan. In addition, the authentic self does not have to be *created* from remnants of the adaptive self in this transformation. The authentic self was created *first*. Its essence has always been within; the adaptive self simply became an alternative — a protective, operating shell, designed to enable the authentic self to act like the conditions it was thrust into, which were incompatible with the authentic self. Because those conditions were left unchallenged — because the authentic self adapted to them — those adaptive choices have now aggregated with a power that threatens humanity. The qualities within the authentic self that retreated from those conditions are now the tool for their reversal. Accordingly, the universal consciousness has provided safe passage and harbor for the return and expression of those qualities, without consequences. On an individual level, that means that you, a person of higher consciousness, are being tapped to experience the power of your own Being, without consequences — summoning the courage, therefore, to express the truth of who you are, what you know, what you feel, what you need and what you are here to do.

The purpose of the adaptive self has been to give you the experience of the pain humanity is in — the denials, fears, patterns and ego indulgences that perpetuate its conditions — and thereby motivate you to contribute to reversing those conditions. Yours is no longer the task of learning from the lessons incurred by the adaptive self. Rather, you are now being given the information and inspiration for how to model the alternative. The lessons of the adaptive self are over. Now your teaching has begun.

Time-honored, karmic conditions have imposed on the evolving consciousness the constant mantra, "What am I to learn from this?" In the quantum consciousness transition, the adaptive self and the authentic self meet in the vortex of exchange and the adaptive self dissolves by transferring to the authentic self that which it has learned from experience. The authentic self is thereafter challenged simply to Be — to access and express the truth. It *knows* the lessons of consequences; they were learned in the adaptive mode. In the authentic mode, however, there are no lessons to learn from Being. Being is the *teacher*. You are therefore to transition into asking of the circumstances you find yourself Being in, "What can I teach? What can I model? What can I say or do to inspire this person/organization to change?" In this manner, the energy of the learning from the adaptive experience is transformed. It becomes the curriculum for teaching, and the information and inspiration for expressing, Being.

DAY NUMBER SEVEN

Guidelines:

Does what I have and what I do reflect
who I am becoming?

This day invites you to look closely at your relationship with the material plane, without judgment, guilt, fear or assumptions about how this program is going to prompt you in that regard. Simply notice, for example, the items you have deemed necessary to your lifestyle . What do they say to you? That you have good taste? That you used your money well? That you have only what you need, and that you live in moderation? Or have you denied yourself things you truly need, even though the universe has given you the resources to have what you need? On the other hand, have you accumulated unnecessarily, or for the wrong reasons? Put another way, do you have what you need or do you have items *instead* of what you need?

The Material Plane

Look also at your relationship with money. Do you pay your bills on time? Do you have excessive charge card debt? (If so, "Debt As a Spiritual Teacher," on page 105 will help transform that debt.) Is your checkbook balanced? Do you save regularly? Adequately? Do you spend within your means? Do you use your money consciously? Do you invest your money consciously? Do you make your own investment decisions? Or turn that power over to someone else?

Do you have any guilt or fear in connection with money? Do you ascribe value to yourself or others based on the money/items you have, or they have? Do you love yourself in the way you relate to money? Are you trustworthy in money matters? Do you make clear, powerful agreements when money is concerned? Do you tip servers, baggage and valet persons, haircutters, etc., appropriately? Do you spend or give based on obligation? Do you donate to organizations or causes that support your values?

Is your relationship with money based on *your* values solely, or are some of your attitudes, patterns, emotions or actions carryovers from your upbringing? Along those lines, do you like your family's values and relationship with money? Do you respect their values? Their way of using money? Do you trust your family in matters pertaining to money? Are they open, generous, unconditionally loving about money? Or secretive, controlling, manipulative and petty?

Summary Question: On a sheet of paper, write your response to the following: Does your relationship with money reflect your authentic self? If so, how? If not, why? And if not, how? And what can you do to change that? ("Examining My Relationship with Money," on page 108 is a good place to start.)

The Physical Plane

Now look at the physical plane and the body, asking first, do you love your body? Do you love *all* of it? If so, why? If not, why? Do you treat it lovingly? Do you relate to your body based on *its* needs or your own? For example, if you work out, is it because you want your physical container to be strong, adept and healthy . . . or is it because your ego wants the credit for the condition your body is in?

(Consider also at this point in this reading, how are you feeling about inventorying these aspects of your life? Do these questions remind you of inadequacies you have felt or others' judgments you have experienced, or can you welcome them as identifying and challenging your untapped power, maturity and accountability . . . because that is the purpose of this inventory.)

Along those lines, look at your food choices. Are they based on your unique body's individualized needs? Or does your ego play a part in what it will or will not allow your body to have? And in this category of body needs, do you cook balanced meals for yourself regularly? Do you eat slowly? Small bites chewed well? Or do you stuff large portions into your mouth non-consciously? When you buy groceries, do you do so thoughtfully, lovingly? Or do you hurry? Select the quickest and easiest? And then throw away items that have spoiled before you had time to cook them? If it is time for you to change any of these patterns, take time to write down what you can begin to do differently.

To continue reflecting on your physical body, consider also these additional aspects of self-care:

Do you look at nutritional content of food items before you buy? Do you consider sodium, fat content, cholesterol, additives, preservatives, chemicals, sugar? Do you sometimes binge? Do you feel the need to hide certain food habits or cravings? Do you use food as a reward? Or do you deny yourself certain foods, or certain portions, for the wrong reasons?

Is your refrigerator clean? Is it orderly? Does it embarrass you for someone to see inside it? Or inside your freezer? Are your cupboards well stocked? Orderly? Do you have the cooking utensils you need? Are they in conscious condition? Do you keep them stored in an orderly manner? Do you wash your dishes regularly? And put them in cupboards, not leaving the dishdrainer constantly filled? Are your sponges, scouring pads, dish towels, potholders, etc., in conscious condition? And is the area under your sink well stocked and orderly? Do you keep an adequate supply of soap, cleanser, paper towels, toilet tissue, toothpaste, shampoo, trash bags . . . things you use regularly? Or do you regularly run out of such items?

Summary Question: Write your response to the following: Does the way you care and provide for your physical body and its needs reflect the authentic or the adaptive self? How?

Within your physical surroundings, is your home orderly? Do you clean regularly? Do you launder regularly, or let everything pile up until the last minute? Do you clean the bathtub, toilets, floors and windows regularly? Do you vacuum, sweep, dust, empty trash, throw away newspapers, magazines, stacks of mail, etc., regularly?

Do you repair what is broken, and replace what is worn out? Do you do so immediately, or procrastinate? Do you promptly return borrowed items? Do you regularly clean out the basement, attic, garage, closets, storage areas, trunk of the car, glove compartment, wallet, purse, briefcase, center desk drawer, stacks of files? In other words:

Summary Question: Write your response to the following: Are you attracting and keeping only what you need, or are you non-consciously accumulating or subconsciously neglecting? Accordingly, what are you ready to change?

Releasing The Gifts

When inventorying these issues in this manner, topics that are not listed above may flash into your consciousness. Thank your soul for those insights and act on them. The types of non-conscious, unproductive aspects cited above require energy to sustain, or avoid. So long as that energy is stored in these patterns, it cannot subsidize the potential awaiting the authentic self. To the contrary, perpetuating these patterns represents a constant reminder of the lack of power, discipline, accountability, self-love and self-respect that the adaptive self has experienced and felt. Most important, however, these conditions are frequently indicators of early life neglect. Individuals who were not loved adequately, or taken care of, did not receive that type and quality of energy into themselves. At this time of your spiritual maturity and development, however, your soul is engaged to provide loving support. Your soul will help you mobilize the will and commitment for you to address these areas that your ego *knows* it is accountable for, and *knows* the feelings of powerlessness or judgment it carries around when not meeting its own standards.

Therefore, in this week that is dedicated to accessing courage, any camouflage concealing that courage, such as habits cited above, must be targeted for transformation. The patterns identified above are not indications of weakness or inadequacy. They are indicators of gifted, creative, wounded potential that has not yet managed to find a way to manifest fully and uniquely. Gaining dominion over the material and physical planes is therefore essential, because the density of those patterns immobilizes the potential that lies within.

For this week that is dedicated toward expressing one's full potential, courage is the key. It is the energy within that mobilizes fearlessly. Thus, as the authentic self gathers the courage and momentum to express its potential, the courage of the adaptive self is extremely important. That self is asked to acknowledge the truth of the patterns it has perpetuated. In the highest form of self-sacrifice, the adaptive self is asked to allow the energy of those patterns it has created and relied on to be released — to empower the authentic and thereby dissolve the power, purpose and potential of the adaptive self.

DAY NUMBER EIGHT

Guidelines:
Radiant energies pour into spaces created
by the ego's willingness.

Since the authentic self is soul-directed and the adaptive self ego-directed, the universe's energies and consciousness are essential to the expression of authenticity. In the instance of day seven's inventory, that is surely true. The universe created the abundance of the third dimension and the material plane because they serve a purpose in the evolution of the ego. They, too, evolve by using their energies in behalf of the ego's evolution. And, in the overall plan of consciousness evolution, it is possible for items or aspects of one's self to evolve their consciousness without sacrifice, without loss, and even without three-dimensional change. The change *can* be purely vibrational . . . and yet in some instances, to release is most powerful.

Messages From Items

One of the most obvious examples is an item or behavior used by the ego to get attention or status. An article of clothing, for example. Perhaps three-dimensionally it *is* quite lovely. It might be expensive. It might look very nice on the person who purchased it. But if it was purchased for attention or status, then to everyone whose ego is not consumed by the emptiness of status, the item emanates pretentiousness. Even if others compliment it — which the adorned ego undoubtedly had in mind — they will do so from the same falseness employed in the purpose of the purchase. The *purpose* for which an item or action is three-dimensionally instituted radiates constantly. It is the truth, regardless of what the ego has concocted and regardless of the ego's fantasies or needs. Thus, others sense the truth of the energy involved in the purpose of the action, or the purchase of the item, irrespective of the energy or effect generated by the ego's intention or need.

The truth of one's authenticity radiates constantly also. Furthermore, the energy of the qualities radiating from an individual positions that person within a certain stratum of consciousness. Persons with similar qualities and consciousness are aggregated on the same level. From the level where inauthentic vibrations collect, it often appears that "everyone" is like this. That (false) conclusion reinforces the ego's disincentive to change, even though the soul is regularly beaming in information (truth) to counter the ego's conclusion. The soul's message is insistent: to attract persons with superior qualities, one must possess those qualities. If the ego tends to reject the soul's guidance to cease the adaptive patterns, it is because the ego sees no hope for its authentic self to function or succeed. On the layer of consciousness hosting the adaptive self that is true: the authentic is incompatible. What the ego does not realize, however, is that the soul knows of levels of consciousness where authentic selves dwell and succeed, and it knows the guidelines for how to reach those other realms. The soul also knows that the ego does not know — either that they exist or how to access them.

Where The Soul Dwells

If the ego's relationship with truth were more powerful, it could know. But the ego attracts the quality and quantity of truth it lives. So a pretentious, inauthentic ego, constantly preoccupied with how it looks or behaves in order to gain others' approval, is not focused on the truth of who it is, what it knows, what it feels, what it needs, or what it is here to do. It is constantly denying such truth, living according to others' standards and expectations, thinking that is its only alternative. And yet, that equivalent of purgatory can end just as soon as the ego stops doing its adaptive routine. At the instant the ego resists perpetuating that self, the soul is then given the space to drop in energy for a new repertoire — one that is authentic. The ego does not know how to create that alternative to itself because it has used up its considerable creativity in the design and manufacture of the adaptive. The soul, however, has access to the fourth dimensional energies. That is where the soul's consciousness dwells. That is also where the universe has stored the energies to be disbursed to the collective consciousness of the Earth plane, penetrating the ego-adaptive and replacing it with soul-directed authentic.

The ego's task is simply to acknowledge the truth and be willing to express it. That is what creates the passageway for exchanging the ego's handiwork for the soul's. When the ego acknowledges the truth of the limited choices it is perpetuating — and the truth that those choices will only continue to produce consequences, regardless of the ego's intent — then those aspects of the adaptive self will have served their purpose: to bring the ego's consciousness back to the truth it has been denying in the adaptive way of behaving. At that instant, truth dissolves the purpose the adaptive self has served and leaves space for the soul to inject into the ego's consciousness an element of authentic, reclaimed potential.

The ego's challenge is to acknowledge the truth of the adaptive self's efforts and consequences, and resist perpetuating them. Each moment the ego opts not to perpetuate the unproductive patterns, even though in that instance it does not have within its repertoire an alternative, the ego's willingness to say no to the patterns creates the space for the soul to intervene. The soul gathers the energies of that pattern, changes their consciousness, and redirects them to create a new, authentic repertoire.

This soul-directed authenticity works magnificently. It is kind, gentle, strong, loving, truthful, powerful, sensitive and courageous. The results it produces are astounding to the ego that has been relying on its scrappy, adaptive self to wing it, moment to moment. As it begins to experience the qualitative difference of the soul's guidance — the soul-directed repertoire that is based on truth and authenticity — the ego realizes that the qualities accompanying the authentic are sustainable. They have integrity. They are qualities which, as the ego feels them gathering within, it knows it can trust.

Once the ego experiences these qualities, it *knows* they are the essence it has been missing, longing for. The ego realizes that its focus on the outward has been hopelessly misguided. It sees how others have been able to see through those outward manifestations even though the ego itself could not allow itself to see that truth. With only glimmers of the power of the authentic self in place, the ego regains hope that there *is* a way for it to be, without consequences; a way for it to Be, rather than constantly having to package itself based on its (often erroneous) assessment of which part of itself would be acceptable under what conditions in the presence of which individuals.

Soul Healing

With its commitment to exchange the adaptive for the authentic, the ego can experience the soul's love and begin to heal. Then the ego's love can extend to and embrace the authentic self as it expresses itself more and more. The authentic self is, indeed, lovable. Its qualities are lovable, and the results it produces are, also. The love that begins to radiate from others matches the radiant love emerging from within. Everything within and around the new self takes on a new vibration — a new consciousness — a new meaning and purpose. At the same time, any thing or any one in one's life that can serve the emerging authentic self will be given an opportunity to adjust its consciousness to match the evolution from adaptive to authentic. Thus, any item needs simply to be asked, "Am I to keep this item because its consciousness has changed along with mine, or has it served its purpose and is to go?" The item will communicate its response. Likewise, significant relationships will adjust to the authentic self. Only in rare circumstances will a relationship be dissolved. If so, that outcome only confirms a truth the ego has denied. Authenticity does not produce loss. Only expansion and transformation.

On this powerful day wherein the ego's willingness creates spaces for radiant energies to pour into, review that which is around you so that the consciousness of all that has come through the adaptive self can evolve to support and complement the authentic self emerging.

DAY NUMBER NINE

Guidelines:

Accessing the Courage to

Express my Full Potential.

In the cosmology writings of Dion Fortune there is a reference to the term "ring pass not." She uses that term to describe dimensions of consciousness that are barred to lower consciousness penetration — dimensions so sacred the universe has provisions for protecting them from the ego's invasion. This day in this program is somewhat "ring pass not." Much has been activated in your consciousness. Truth is stirring up the patterns you have both lamented and perpetuated. However, this program's purpose far exceeds simply stirring up. Its promise is to awaken and unleash. And in this particular week the focus is on your potential and the energies that keep it locked within.

Challenging The Familiar

Your soul is rearranging energies in your subconscious and unconscious and asking the ego to trust the expression of the truth within. The soul knows how difficult it is to access and trust that truth. But the soul also knows the angst the ego feels as it edits, compromises and holds back. In some instances the pain is so familiar it does not even register as pain any more. Restricting the self's expression of how it truly feels and what it earnestly needs is so automatic by now that that action completely bypasses the feelings and needs that are present. The ego may have resigned itself to the conclusion that its challenge is to manage this restrictive condition as best it can. But that clearly is not the universe's plan. Those restrictive conditions are to be transformed, yielding their energies to create opportunities to express your potential.

The universe has placed within your ego's access both powerful, inspiring soul communication and also great courage. They are to bar lower levels of consciousness from sabotaging your potential — not only to salvage your own gifts and creativity, but equally important, to ensure that the purpose of your own restrictions is served. You are to break out of those limitations so that you contribute to the reversal of conditions that restrict others' potential as well. This is your role: to register in the collective consciousness the information and inspiration for others to find and follow. Accordingly, the universe has positioned you strategically and purposefully to impact the persons and situations around you at this moment of your own significant change. You are to bring to them first, and the collective as a result, the catalytic interactions that break up restrictive patterns and reassemble their energy to express untapped potential.

No Consequences

It is especially important that you feel the truth of this purpose and potential and fear no consequences. Today, therefore, you will be given an opportunity to test this assignment, to assure yourself that it is both safe and divinely intended that this restrictive period give way to purpose, potential, and unprecedented access to Being. Other lives and circumstances have gathered around you to benefit from your courage and initiating action, so now is the time, and

Reclaiming the Authentic Self

you are the activator. As you Be in accordance with your soul's guidance, that spark of courage and inspiration will ignite others . . . but not because you consciously, willfully intend it or direct it. Being is not intention. It is not willed. Those are ego-based and ego-controlled. Being is soul-directed. It is that expression others are awaiting.

At this time of courageous activation from within, you are not to allow doubt or fear or procrastination to control this energy. It must be used. It must be trusted. You are part of a planetary awakening of this energy and the potential it is dedicated to activate. Thus, when your moment arrives, your ego must do as all egos at this moment are destined to do: take a deep breath and allow your Being to come forward. From the cosmos, looking down onto this Earth plane phenomenon, you activate your link in the cosmic chain of creative potential being unleashed . . . and the activation mechanism is courage. The courage to Be.

Because this is part of the universe's plan for evolving human consciousness through soul-directed expression, the universe has provided "ring pass not"-type barricades to the ego's will and denial. Thus, on this day when numerous circumstances have been convened to benefit from the courage you are to manifest, if you bypass one, the imperative will only intensify. The next opportunity will be even more challenging — and essential. The universe's unlimited resources enable it to orchestrate as many situations as your ego requires to engage its courage and express its potential.

This willingness to surge past the typical constraints in the ego's condition are part of your own very evolved soul's service to humanity. You are asked to summon the courage within because the truth is that you *know* it is there. Thus, the risks your ego might concoct and fantasize in order to defer or deny are only a byproduct of typical ego restriction. Anything produced by the ego in this manner is contrary to the truth and therefore has no integrity. Yet, it is the myriad of such ego-based restrictions on this planet that you are being asked to help dissolve: ego-based doubts, not founded on truth, fueled by fantasies, fears and projections, wholly lacking in integrity . . . yet so powerful that enormous creativity and potential is immobilized as a result.

You are asked to know the truth of such restrictions — that they are not as powerful as the potential within you because the restrictions are not founded on truth. Your potential is. But the key to exchanging the power those restrictions have had, for the power your Being can express, lies with your ego. Will it continue to perpetuate the restrictions because they are familiar — or will it access the courage to express your potential because that is the truth of who you are, what you know and what you are here to do? Your soul is asking only that you acknowledge and express the truth you have known.

No Fear

To assist, this program is assuring you that fearing the consequences of that truth is no longer a viable excuse for the ego to withhold that potential. It is the truth, and there are no consequences to truth. The energy of truth as it comes through the courage within you will literally dissolve and transform anything constructed with less than the truth — including automatic, restrictive patterns that have held you in check for years. Those conditions and situations are part of the human condition the universe is finally directing energies into the collective consciousness to dissolve. Those conditions are ready for transformation; they are waiting for that evolutionary opportunity: they have served their purpose in their present state and are prepared to be transformed to their next level of service in the evolution of human consciousness. You are the activator. You do not have to convince. You just Be. The universe will do the rest.

In the universal plan, *many* conditions that lack integrity will be given the option to make a higher choice — and many will respond. They will already know their values are vulnerable. They will have felt the tremors in the collective consciousness signaling the redistribution of power and resources based on the greatest good for the greatest number. They will know they must change, but they may not know how. They may need a demonstration of the necessary courage, and the positive outcome to expressing the truth. Then, when they witness it, experience it and benefit from it, they, too, will get the message: now is the time — this is the way.

DAY NUMBER TEN

Guidelines:

To Be or Not to Be is still the question.

Truth is the word humanity uses to describe the information that comes to the ego from the creator consciousness directly through the soul as intuition. Within the dynamics of a lifetime, the ego attracts the quality and quantity of truth it lives. In principles of evolution, the longer a soul has been in this universe, the greater its experience of truth. Thus, an old soul will have greater access to truth than a less evolved soul.

The Matrix

The degree to which an individual ego accesses truth is incidental to the manner in which truth *manifests*. It manifests completely and constantly every moment. The total truth of any incident, utterance or thought is fully manifested every instant. However, if truth is viewed as a matrix — an enormous Rubik cube with countless cubicles — then even though the entire matrix contains the complete truth, if an ego's relationship with truth is compromised, then that ego will only access *part* of the truth. That ego's consciousness will beam part way into that matrix and illuminate a limited number of the cubicles, but the entire truth will not be revealed because the ego's consciousness is limited in its own relationship to truth.

Because truth is constantly and fully present each moment, however, it is important to recognize that the ego must employ some subconscious mechanism to cloud — or some unconscious mechanism in order totally to block — the truth that is constantly present. Those lower consciousness patterns were originally constructed in relation to truth; therefore they are perpetuated in relation to truth, and they must be addressed and transformed in relation to the truth of the authentic self and the power of Being without consequences.

The Birth Of The Adaptive Self

Truth is humanity's source of power and love is humanity's emotional reward for its relationship with truth. Thus, the quality and quantity of truth in one's life determines the quality and quantity of love — universal love, self-love and love in connection with others. In order for the ego to have constructed lower consciousness patterns in relation to truth, at some point in early life it must have experienced that the truth of its Being was not lovable, or acceptable, or valuable. As a result, the ego also would have suffered the consequences of unlove. Concluding that its true self was unlovable or not valuable, and yet, knowing it needed love and some form of value to negotiate its lifetime on Earth, the ego inevitably scrambled to identify what others did in order to get love, or to be valued. Then it valiantly struggled to present itself accordingly. Thus, the adaptive self was born: a creation of the ego's efforts to find love.

One of the greatest consequences of the adaptive self is, however, that it has never experienced love at the level of its true self. Furthermore, it experienced a consequence of Being its true self: it was unloved. But because the adaptive self has not attracted love through its adaptation efforts either, the conditioned ego has experienced both its authentic self and its adaptive self unable to attract the love it needs.

It is this crisis situation that calls in the soul and the universal plan for restoring the authentic self with the experience of truth and love. Otherwise, the ego cannot attract the love it needs while operating in the adaptive manner because it will be attracted to, and attractive to, persons operating the same way. Thus, the ego's needs for love are never met, its disappointments increase, it feels continually alienated and insecure, and its need for love intensifies with each effort that sabotages that need. In addition, the ego can never come close to expressing its potential because of the turbulence generated from needing and not finding love.

Because this condition is so abundant on this planet at this time, you may experience your own effort to Be, interacting on that same plane with much of humanity that is not able to Be, as outwardly somewhat like the above description. But deep within, Being both feels and *is* totally different. It is therefore vitally important that your own commitment to Being not be waylaid or dissuaded by the extenuating circumstances around you. You do have this capacity. You do have this assignment. And the universe is pouring energies through your soul and into your adaptive self to create the exchange of its energies for the experience of authentic Being.

Know, therefore, that even as your soul releases and supports your authentic Being, you will still encounter people and situations that are incompatible with your Being. However, in the past, your adaptive self often denied or ignored the incompatibilities because it needed to find love and acceptance. Now, in an instant you will see how the truth of who you are and the truth of who they are is incompatible with your Authentic Being. And that will be the challenge: to assess and accept the incompatibility and keep moving, discriminating and seeking the quality of truth and love that meets your standards and needs. Inside you is the power to sustain your Being. It is *divinely* sustained now, unlike when it first tried to come forward in early life. Then you did not have the capacity, as a child, to hold onto it in the midst of influential others, whom you desperately needed, but who were unable to appreciate and love the power of your Being. There are still differences in your Being and others . . . but no consequences. You are not abandoning the truth of who you are, thereby requiring a set of lessons to return you to that truth. Consequences result only when the truth has been manipulated or denied, requiring lessons to bring you back to the original truth. ("Questions Related to My Relationship with Love," on page 111 will help you see more clearly the quality and quantity of love in your life.)

Being Attracts Being

As you now discriminate among those who can respond to your Being, and those who cannot, the very fact of your Being illuminates the matrix of truth and thereby enables you to feel the power of knowing why something or someone is not the highest option for you at this time. Then, because you are filled with that knowing, you do not need anything else from that situation. You simply move on to the next. Because the capacity to Be begets the capacity to know, even if moving on is difficult, the reward within will be in knowing: knowing who you are and what you need; knowing who and what meets your needs; and, as always, having the courage to act in relation to that knowing.

The truth also fully illuminates the potential within, as well as the potential in connection with another person or a situation. The ego's challenge is to experience, courageously, that potential, not needing or deluding itself that there is more — not shying away from all that there is. Experiencing all that there is, then moving on, sometimes to the next moment, sometimes to the next meeting, and sometimes to the next relationship, never looking back unless there is new information available from the soul relative to that which you have moved beyond . . . that is the perpetual challenge of Being in the midst of humanity. That is also the method for moving steadily toward that portion of humanity who is also Being. The ultimate reward therefore is both to Be and to connect with those whose courage, creativity and authenticity you can create and Be with.

Being fully present in the truth at any given moment ensures against the need for looking back, lamenting, being disappointed or angry. If those reactions to the past are recalled without accompanying any new insights into the past, they are covering up truths about the past that the ego is resisting at the moment it chooses those options to truth. It therefore never serves the ego to ruminate, dwell on, or continuously think about a situation from the past by only going over and over what already occurred. Such lower consciousness preoccupations inevitably function to keep significant new information from coming forth. In response to those old patterns, the authentic self courageously intercepts them by asking: What is the truth? If no awareness presents itself, the ego must cease the preoccupation.

Electing to fill one's thoughts by resurrecting old information is electing "Not to Be." Thus, unless a new insight brings you back to that past event, the present and its truth and challenges are the only place "To Be."

DAY NUMBER ELEVEN

Guidelines:

Be, today, and receive the results.

DAY TWELVE

Guidelines:

Experiencing the power of Being,

without consequences.

Whereas yesterday's energies produced a subtle demonstration of how the outside world is going to receive your refined, authentic self, the guidelines for today are deeper and more specific. The *power* of Being is in the truth. Thus, a truth will either emerge from or settle within your consciousness today, indicating the direction your "no consequences" self is to take.

The topic may be money. Or relationship. It could be career, family, health, or emotional security. To be useful, today's challenge must be in an area that regularly takes a toll on your Being . . . an area wherein you regularly give up your power by not being willing to express the truth of who you are, what you feel, what you need, or what you know. Prepare for today's challenge by trusting the universe to dissolve a barrier between you and truth, and allow the universe to clear the path for your internal strength to register a success in expressing the truth, without consequences.

If the barrier that must be dissolved is a familiar subconscious pattern such as doubt or fear, then the ego must rigorously devote itself to soul guidance today, letting only the truth prevail. In the presence of doubt, which is the ego's most formidable weapon against truth, the ego lapses into patterns that first assaulted its relationship with truth . . . undoubtedly pertaining to the truth of its own value and potential.

Reclaiming Your Worth

Now the ego must challenge any doubts and untruths about its worth. It must also verify whether its fears that emerge now are based on truth (which at this point in this program is unlikely) or whether they are projections still carried forth from early life situations. For the next days of this program, your ego is quite personally and specifically challenged to change the memory of such beliefs held inside. You are challenged instead to express the truth of your divinely created Being and to experience the power of *your* valuing who that is. You are to allow *your* value to override others' evaluation of you. (Because your self-worth may be defined or affected by your career, refer to "Questions Related to My Work Environment," on page 114.)

You can now feel the power surging inside to become the sole authority for your values, worth, purpose and potential. The universe has distributed undifferentiated energy onto the Earth plane for this purpose. Those potent energies are waiting to be gathered unto the ego that releases the old and prepares to create the new. The ego can know that any barriers and restrictions occurring in its life have been outward manifestations of the barriers and restrictions to its Being. But once the truth of that Being begins to expand from within, those barriers and restrictions are dissolved. In their place, the universe allocates energy to manifest according to gifts, talents, potential, and the unfolding of one's purpose.

Irrespective of cause/effect — and regardless of what might have been one's patterns and logical potential in the past — this way of Being is brought in from the higher planes and assembled according to the universe's specifications. The ego that has been restricted does not have to perpetuate those restrictions. Its liberation comes by asking "What is the truth?" Are those beliefs from the past accurate? Are others' past assessments valid now? Am I still to be in relationship with someone who views me this way? And if I am, how can I change the relationship so that it does not perpetuate these patterns that refute the truth?

In response, your ego will either be shown how to dissolve the patterns or it will be shown a truth from within that will replace them.

In each instance in the past that produced consequences, the ego in some way compromised or denied the truth. Notwithstanding the fact that it was vulnerable or that circumstances left it no choice, the truth is that the ego did not operate at the truest expression of itself . . . and there were consequences.

Now the ego is asked to review those consequences and acknowledge/reclaim the truth that was compromised. This exercise is important now because in this program, energies similar to those circumstances will revisit. This time the ego will be able to access the courage and truth that are now available within, and it can co-create a different outcome.

For this purpose, any such restrictive conditions that have reappeared in your life during this program are to be welcomed and valued. They are not the product of previous patterns. They are not the restrictive, self-defeating outcomes set in motion by the adaptive, struggling self. These representative situations have manifested only for the authentic self to confront and replace them based on its new way of Being and its new qualities within.

Reclaiming Your Power

Remaining mindful that there now are no consequences to its Being, the ego will be invited to revisit the patterns it has previously given power to. Once it prevails, it will reclaim that power and add to its new repertoire the self-respect and self-love for having done so. Revisiting and transforming its previous patterns does involve the reappearance of certain patterns the ego may have thought were eliminated. But the ego flushes them out now only because their residual energies do linger and would eventually reappear. In this instance, however, they are not the consequence of former self-defeating patterns. Their appearance now is positive. It means the new strength within you is first being used to dip further into lower consciousness patterns to completely eliminate and transform them. This experience is a testament to your growth, therefore — not failure.

Your ego will now have in its own consciousness the experience of confronting these patterns and transforming them on its own. Thus, it will know it has in its own repertoire the strength and capacity to transform any remaining obstacles to expressing its full potential. Your ego will know that its own role in ceasing the unproductive behavior allows the soul to create an alternative . . . and this newfound power and joy will perpetuate because it is soul-directed.

Dissolving The Patterns

To assist the ego in this process, an exercise in writing and transmuting any residue of those patterns can be helpful today. On four separate sheets of paper write the following:

On page one: What are the consequences I experienced in the past when I expressed the truth of who I am?

On page two: What are the consequences I am experiencing now as I perpetuate the patterns that developed as a result, and eventually became my adaptive self?

On page three: What is the truth I know within in connection with how these patterns and their consequences are restricting my purpose and my potential?

On page four: Divide this page into two columns.
Column One: What are my doubts or fears in connection with expressing my authentic self?
Column Two: (Beside each of the entries in Column One write this response.) How can my adaptive self   give way to my authentic self so that its Being is free of these doubts or fears?

If this exercise requires more than one sitting, be patient if your ego is resistant to replacing the adaptive self it has masterfully created as an essential survival tool. The power of this day is in seeing the truth of the past and its consequences . . . while knowing the truth of the changes underway.

DAY NUMBER THIRTEEN

Guidelines:

When much is given, much is asked.

As emissary of quantum vs. linear evolution, the Aquarian ego is given an extraordinary role: to access and express a dimension of consciousness that transcends and dissolves the conditions and consequences in the wake of the Karmic system. Part of that dissolving involves the ego consciously participating in the transformation of its own patterns by acknowledging the truth of their origin, their purpose, their consequences, and the soul's directive for ceasing them.

From the written exercise of yesterday, an addendum is attached. Today you are to read aloud each entry from the written exercise and, as you do so, draw a line through any entries you are ready to release. On a new page, write those released entries, then burn the page and flush the ashes . . . asking aloud, as you do so, that the energy so transmuted return to you as awareness to serve the powerful expression of your authentic self. You must also commit to honoring the information that comes back to you.

In addition, to release any other energy trapped in unproductive patterns, examine the following daily life routines to determine whether they are serving their highest potential:

Assessing The Familiar

Physical

If you have worn your hair the same way — or been going to the same haircutter for a long time — it may be time to change. In the Samson tradition, hair reflects power. When a haircutter takes more of your hair than you have given permission, that indicates that in some aspect of your life, you are giving up your power. In addition, hair that is too long reflects dependency, which is also a compromise of one's power.

Shampoos, soaps, toothpaste, comb and brush, shaving cream, cosmetics, lotions, deodorants . . . all body care items are to be examined carefully to ensure they represent your new vibration. Likewise, if you have kept them in the same place for a long time, rearrange their locations to free up that fixed energy field.

Sheets, towels, underwear, sleepwear, robes, socks . . . check out their energy. It may be used up. Having supported your old vibration, these items' energies may have been consumed. They also may be subject to the depreciated ego: if no one sees them, then it is all right for them to be ragged and worn. But that is so not true of the newly-valued self. And it can be non-complementary to that new self to have it using sheets and towels from, for example, a former marriage. The same may be true for the mattress. Or furniture. Dishes, jewelry, photos, clothing . . . it is time for *everything* to be evaluated carefully and consciously. It may not need to be replaced; or it may have to continue serving until funds to replace it are available. But each item that is to stay must be newly contracted with the newly-emerging self. It is important to inventory everything in one's surroundings and possession and ask if it is to remain in its existing location, be moved or be replaced. (The "Questions Related to My Home Environment," on page 117 will contribute to this evaluation.)

Since excess is one of the clues of unmanaged needs, the authentic self knows what it needs and what it does not need, and it has the courage to act in accordance with those needs. It has the power to find a perfect place for its excess items to be of use: garage sale, friend, battered women's center, Goodwill, etc. The authentic self especially needs to be released from items from the past since they met the needs of the adaptive self, not the authentic.

In the area of food, this is another opportunity to look in the refrigerator and cupboards and see if they reflect the most loving, powerful, conscious care of the emerging authentic self. Particularly in relation to vitamins and supplements, the question is whether they are serving the body or the ego. If they are the ego's substitute for conscious care, then they are minimally effective in addressing an issue of neglect. Also, if there are so many that they send the body into chaos trying to absorb, assimilate and disburse their energies, that too, bears examination.

Emotional

Hidden symptoms of anger may be masking the authentic, purposeful expression of that emotion: arriving late, frequent job changes, unsustainable relationships, accumulated clutter, preoccupation with the past, unopened mail, speeding, parking tickets, excessive talking, lost items, procrastination, telling lies, forgetting, misplacing, not returning phone calls, bounced checks, unpaid bills, regimented order, unrealistic expectations, sarcasm, "accidents," burned food, burns to the skin, running out of gas, not enough time, frequent illness, cuts, scratches, fever, inflammation, excessive eating, drinking, spending or accumulating. In the above instances, pay attention to whatever subconscious thoughts are occupying your consciousness at the time of these routine behaviors. Because anger is related to an unmet need for love, these clues will enable you to untangle these energies and redirect them toward a more reliable supply of love.

It is also helpful to look at your relationship with fear, and the ways it may be manifesting. As one of the four principal emotions (love, anger, fear, sadness), fear does have a purpose — to let us know when our life is in danger. Any other fear is based on anger that has accumulated to the degree that its intensity is overwhelming our connection with love. Thus, the ego's fear is that its buildup of anger will keep it from attracting the love that it needs. And the longer the anger and fear hang around, the more love *is* jeopardized, ultimately producing a supply of sadness. That sadness results from the loss connected with the self . . . which did not express itself truthfully. Therefore, it compromised, lost self-respect, self-love, power, and also lost hope of attracting the love it needs.

To reverse this pattern requires acknowledging, expressing and releasing the sadness. That release leads into the anger that has been accumulated toward others. Now it can be directed toward those aspects of the self that are adaptive vs. authentic and therefore unable to attract the love and healing which the adaptive self requires. In this process of challenging patterns that hold the former self in place, the energy to Be is released.

Willingness To Change

As you evaluate the habits and items reflecting your needs, values and experiences up to this point in your lifetime, know that insights and change, not loss, is the objective. Items, habits, persons, situations . . . having been attracted to and attractive to your adaptive self, they may find the adjustment to your authentic self difficult. It is *possible* they will not continue. But to speculate is wasteful because you do not know. And you can be assured that the least likely in your mind can be the most likely to stay according to the universe's plan. So let everything Be to *its* highest potential as well. If a relationship has fully served you and its purpose in your life, it will be released. If there is more to teach or learn or evolve, the other person will take cues from you and access potential within just as you are doing. Together you will have even more joy and meaning to express.

If some thing or some one has contributed all that is possible, the change that ensues will leave space and awareness to enable you to attract what you now need. In this period of change, look within first, expecting the resources to create the changes you need to be there or to be accessible and available through your soul. Releasing the grid of habits, items, expectations and needs accumulated by the adaptive self enables the soul to illuminate that space with awareness and new capacity.

This energy transformation is exciting. The creative handiwork of the soul is impressive. And the potential revealed within and around is indeed a testament to the unique, creative, valued self that is emerging with meaning and purpose.

DAY NUMBER FOURTEEN

Guidelines:

The allocations from the universe are adequate
and perfect.

Today you are challenged to experience the timing and balance of the universe's allocation of energy. As a result, you are challenged to release the ego's penchant for planning as a causative factor in manifestation on Earth, and to view the ego's role as co-creative instead. As a result, your ego is likely to encounter an experience today that, if you could choose, you would not plan. On a soul level you *have* chosen this experience, however, to serve the divine plan in some way. Thus, your ego will be tapped accordingly today.

The Ego In Service

Adjusting to the universe's timing is constantly critical to attracting and stewarding the resources for the authentic self. Today is likely to contain at least one significant experience to test the ego's willingness to follow soul guidance and be unattached to, as well as unaffected by, the outcome.

The keyword for today is allocation — universal allocation. The ego's challenge is to identify and express the energies specifically allocated to it, in their timing and in honor of their purpose. The ego is to know that its courage to Be — which is soul-directed — will be activated to serve the universal plan, which is not ego-directed. Thus, the ego is not to refuse or deny or alter today's guidance, even if it would feel more comfortable and safe doing so. Given the challenge of this day, the ego might prefer not being involved, because it is likely to be engaged as an agent of another ego's change.

Universal energies allocated for the purpose of eliminating certain ego-based conditions on this planet must nevertheless be registered through certain *individual* egos, however, because those individual egos are the principal Earth registrar for changes directed at the *collective* ego. The ego subscribing to soul direction is no longer working only in its own interest. It will be utilized as an instrument of other egos' change.

The soul-directed authentic self thereby becomes the equivalent of the role its own soul assumes: it becomes an instrument for directing into others' consciousness an expression of the information and inspiration that will enable them to undergo similar transformation. To serve in this manner the ego must very carefully identify and follow the energies allocated for this purpose. It must trust that its role and representations at those times will fulfill its service, although not necessarily serve itself.

The ego serving this purpose is cautioned not to worry or wonder what others might think or do or how they might react to its other-ego-directed role. Ideally it is not even to care, in the typical ego sense, whether it is liked or listened to in this instance. Its message will definitely be heard by the other ego. That is what matters. Thus, in serving this role today, you are to scrutinize only your ego's expression of the guidance from its soul. And in that instance, the question is: Did your ego register the universe's energies in the timing and manner the universe allocated?

If for some reason your ego did elect on its own to affect the timing or the manner, then that ego resistance to allowing the universe's energies to flow through it created a jammed effect. The individual ego serving the evolution of consciousness is to learn how to avoid that condition. The universal energies *are* going to manifest, *as* intended; so the ego's resistance only creates more intensity and force from the universe. The ego's resistance to the universe's allocation of energies is also the culprit when the ego seems to run out of time. And, because the ego is to serve the universal plan, it must be aligned with the universe's allocation of energies. This means the ego must understand time because it represents the order in which the universe allocates energy onto the Earth plane.

Time

Above all, time is *not* the fourth dimension. Time and the fourth dimension are two constructs, neither of which the human consciousness could figure out, so it declared them to be one and the same. The fourth dimension is the reservoir of energies disbursed onto the third dimension by the soul. Those energies manifest outside the parameters of cause/effect, logic or reason.

Time, on the other hand, is the word humanity uses to describe the orderly utilization of universal energies. It is a construct that exists only in the band of human consciousness surrounding Earth. Out into the cosmos, time has no effect; it has no role. Out there, everything that is is understood for what it is. Accordingly, the universe allocates onto the Earth plane both the quality and quantity of energy necessary to create everything that is to occur on Earth — on the physical, material, intellectual, emotional, psychological, spiritual and mental planes. That spectrum of allocation is beyond the soul's dominion over fourth dimensional energies. Allocating the energy for *everything* on Earth is the universal consciousness at work.

Humanity, in its need to put the universe into (its own) perspective, determined that the universal energies are always the same — seconds, minutes, hours, days, etc. As humanity has experienced, however, some days are longer — some are shorter. Some weeks fleet by. Others seem to drag insufferably. In actuality, the universe allocates much more energy into some moments, hours, days, etc., than others, depending on what needs to be learned.

Time is the word that describes humanity's understanding of the plan that allocates the energy to create on the Earth plane. Therefore, unless the energy has been allocated from the universe, something the ego simply wants it will not be able to obtain. The human ego cannot summon or create on its own the energy to cause something to manifest on Earth. It *attracts* the energy necessary to create all the experiences necessary to accomplish its purpose, and all the lessons essential to its evolution. The ego can wish for, visualize, master mind, intend, treasure map, meditate and affirm only as a co-creative effort. None of those efforts can obtain anything not already allocated; they can only hone the ego's consciousness into doing the preparation for receiving whatever the universe has allocated. The ego has an opportunity, in other words, to identify and release the obstacles to its receiving and manifesting. The ego's efforts do not cause — but they can help identify what is obstructing — that which the ego is to have. And, only when the ego is truly attuned to what it is to have does it meditate, ask for, expect, etc., only and precisely that which is registered already in its name.

Accountability

The challenge for this day, therefore, is to refine the ego's utilization of time/energy, particularly in connection with the principle of accountability: when the soul directs the ego to do something, all the time/energy necessary to accomplish that task is allocated at that time. Thus, to clean the litter box as you are rushing out the door to an important business meeting could be either self-defeating or accountable, depending on the universe's allocation. On the one hand, if a subconscious pattern kicks in, then you will be late and compromise an opportunity. If you are responding to soul guidance, however, there will be time to clean the litter box *and* get to the meeting on time — without breaking the speed limit.

Today you are asked to steward the energy allocated to and through you as the universe directs. In that cooperation with the universal plan, significant insights will be obtained.

DAY NUMBER FIFTEEN

Guidelines:

Managing the Ego, Empowering the Soul.

Spiritually, the ego's challenge is doubt and denial. Materially, its challenge is money. And physically, its challenge is sexuality. Doubt and denial are weapons against truth, and love is humanity's emotional reward for its relationship with truth. Money is often used in place of love. Money also frequently mirrors information about one's relationship with love. When one's sexuality is used to attract love — instead of being a way to express love — then the potential for love is compromised and the ecstasy of sexuality is foreclosed.

At this point in the program, the ego is asked to look directly and intimately into its relationship with love, money, sexuality, doubt, denial and truth — primarily because certain energies in those areas are to be released so that they integrate more fully into the ego's potential. Accordingly, the conditions that hold those energies in place must be examined, starting with needs.

Love And Needs

Although certain spiritual belief systems encourage the transcendence or elimination of needs, from the ego's perspective, its purpose for being on Earth is to experience love; and love is humanity's automatic emotional response when its needs are met. (Anger is humanity's automatic emotional response when its needs are *not* met; thus the disruptive energy of anger is designed to interact in the environment to challenge any untapped potential to express love. "I need to feel your love" is the hidden message of anger.)

The vibration of one's needs distinguishes that individual from all others; and certain needs, which can be met only by certain people, bring individuals together. In a relationship, for example, each individual has various needs. Some can be filled in that relationship; some cannot. Some needs can be met sometimes, not always. The relationship inevitably contains dynamics that specifically do not meet one's needs. But if a person denies his/her needs, or pretends the needs are being met when they are not, then the truth is manipulated and the outcome is compromised.

Humanity's need for love is the gyrating momentum that leads us to one another. If all our needs for love were met in one place at one time, we would stay there. Indeed, our early life environment was specifically inadequate to meet certain of our needs. If all our needs had been met at home, we would still be with those people. Instead, some needs were specifically not met in our home environment so that the impetus of those needs mobilized us to connect with friends, teachers, employers, partners, etc.

Knowing what our needs are, and how to meet those needs, is an important aspect of Being. Even needs we do not like must be honored until they transform. We must accept those needs rather than judge them, knowing that they are messengers about our relationship with love. The more love we have in our life, the greater our capacity to meet our own needs or to manage them. Love is the creative emotion. It will create the dynamics to meet or manage our needs so long as we are living the truth of our authentic self. (The "Inventory of Needs," on page 119 will assist you in assessing the important relationships in your life.)

Money And Sexuality

If our need for love gets mixed up in an area like money or sexuality, then the real, underlying need can never be met. We can, of course, pretend to be in love to be financially taken care of, or we might use our sexuality to avoid being alone. However, in that process we may go through a lot of money and a lot of relationships and still not know what our needs are . . . or how to get them met. At the same time, we will employ denial on an hourly basis in order to avoid the truth of the emptiness, fear and self-contempt that inevitably arise from such desperate efforts. Admittedly, money and sexuality may momentarily anesthetize the pain and fear of not having enough love in our life; but each time we use our dominion over those choices, in defiance of the truth, then we give up our power, lose self-respect, and thereby create a greater *loss* of love — self - love. The truth is, neither money nor sex, as aspects of humanity's experience on Earth, can meet the need for love because they cannot *create* love. They are to be a reflection and expression of love. Only with a foundation of love can money and sexuality become elements of creativity. But when money and sexuality are misused, they cannot serve that purpose.

Together, love and sexuality create life itself, and love and money create the environment in which life can be joyful and thrive. On the other hand, money used to create without love begets an entirely different product; and sexuality as a substitute for love also produces, and perpetuates, an outcome that basically needs, not gives. If the truth about one's relationship with money is denied, then the money's power is misused. Especially when money and love are entangled, money that is used in place of love is virtually wasted. It has no enduring power, or integrity, and the true purpose of money is thereby violated. Nothing purchased, given, or received under those circumstances has any lasting benefit. It can only momentarily cover up the pain within someone giving or receiving under those terms.

The expression of our sexuality can also be empty and wasted unless it is aligned with our needs and connected with love. That is not to say that individuals must love each other in order to enjoy intimacy. Two individuals whose self-love is intact can experience intimacy for the sexual pleasure so long as their needs are managed and their relationship with love is not confused with sexual needs and pleasure. Ideally, however, one's needs are so sufficiently met and/or managed that sexuality can be expressed for its highest purpose — to be humanity's most intense, ecstatic expression of love.

When Needs Change

Because needs, when they are met, open the gateway to love, when a relationship has been inventoried and tested to identify all the needs it can and cannot meet, then its love potential can be assessed. Based on the types of needs it meets, and the depth to which it meets them, the relationship can then be defined and consummated based on its capacity to meet certain needs . . . and its capacity to expand and adapt as needs change. For example, a relationship that tries to be erotic may ultimately have the potential only for friendship; and one that starts platonically may actually evolve into a sexual union. Needs in other areas of life function similarly. A job that is creative and stimulating may become boring and routine; an expensive dream house may become a burden. As individuals change, needs change. Thus, the truth and integrity in a relationship are essential to ensure that the presence and purpose of the love and the needs are constant. The more needs are met, the more love results. The more love, the greater capacity for flexibility and change.

Since an individual's security is constant if based on integrity and love, even if a relationship changes, that person's self-love is a constant and, therefore, a foundation for enduring the relationship change. If a relationship ceases, it is because each person has expressed and experienced all the love that relationship can create. When that moment comes, even though there may be some sadness, the joy of the love exchanged is present and enduring, and the truth of the relationship's closure is a powerful basis for transition. Anger endures, however, if one has denied the truth of the relationship's inadequacy to meet one's needs.

In your own life, review your relationships and your needs. Review your use of money, your sexuality, your dependencies, your integrity. Use this day to inventory these important areas to ensure that your truth and authenticity are expressed to your fullest potential.

DAY NUMBER SIXTEEN

Guidelines:
Plummeting into the truth breaks the seal
to your potential.

The dynamics of day fifteen are designed to loosen energies stored in patterns no longer serving you. The truths and feelings that emerge from those patterns may seem overwhelming. The ego may conclude that regardless of how hard it has tried and how many changes it has made, old patterns still have a grip — still take a toll — still restrict the authentic self and its potential.

Old Barriers: New Possibilities

In this program, at this time, a confluence of universal energies is gathering to assist the ego in its effort to penetrate the barriers to its potential. At times, the momentum that seizes the ego may not feel so productive, however. In some areas, it may feel like that same downward, hopeless spiral into awareness, but not change. Indeed, as the ego slides once again into examining its needs, behaviors and restrictive conditions, at first it may see the terrain unchanged from its other excursions. But that is not the case. Something is definitely different. Opportunities have been positioned in the periphery of the ego's path. They are new opportunities, positioned by the soul, offering new and different potential. They have gathered as the ego has been undergoing insight transformation.

The ego may not yet be aware of these differences and opportunities, however, because it may be preoccupied in an unproductive manner. What is likely to have the ego's attention is the energy of patterns flushed out in the dynamics of this program. The ego may feel in some areas that it has lost ground. It may feel shaky in relation to aspects of its life it thought were in place. Under these circumstances the ego is once again challenged to know the truth and not be affected by that which is not true. If something was indeed in place it will remain so, and it certainly can survive some accountable scrutiny. If something truly was not firmly in place, at least that truth is revealed and the ego can now make adjustments.

Whose Truth?

The distinction is in the truth of the *presence* vs. the content of whatever the ego might be concerned about. The ego may be bombarded by insecurities and judgments from the past. If they are present, the question is, are they the truth? The ego has undoubtedly avoided this excursion into these depths of certain insecurities because it could not bear the "truth" etched deep inside by others. However, experiencing the fact that those "truths" are present — so that they can be survived and overlaid with the ego's *own* truths — that is totally different from succumbing to them *as truth*. And that is what this day in this program is designed to do. It enables the ego to expel others' truths and replace them with its own.

If the ego is therefore willing to spiral downward with this momentum, then it can fall with sufficient force to break the seal on its potential. Its untapped potential will then geyser up and take the ego into the realms it feared it would never reach, especially by dipping further into the truth. But that is the plunge that is required.

The ego had held onto the belief that its extraordinary potential would surely be jeopardized if these "truths" were known . . . while just the opposite is true. Only when those judgmental, erroneous projections by others are expelled can the ego's true potential be released — primarily because its potential is too extraordinary to be expressed by anything operating with those judgments intact.

Understandably, the ego may have interpreted its downward spiral to expel these energies — and the feelings accompanying that journey — as negative. The ego may have feared being lost in those old feelings, even as new insights came through as a result of facing those feelings. The ego nevertheless may have felt it "should" be elsewhere — coping "better."

Once it reaches the bottom with sufficient force, however, it will be lifted to the level of opportunity and functioning the releasing and awareness have created. All along the ego knew it did not know how to get to these energies: both those that *restricted* its potential as well as those that *contained* it. The ego's tendency was to fear that the more it uncovered within, the further it was heading in the opposite direction from being in its fullest potential. Doubting it would have the resources and stamina to climb from the bottom back up to the top, by itself, on its own, the ego denied or avoided self-doubts and insecurities it knew were present, even as it knew they were not based on truth. No wonder, then, that this program took the ego into those chambers of others' labels, indictments and limited thinking to replace them with truth.

Although it may not be aware of the source of this excavating dynamic, the ego's inner momentum is integrity. . . because authenticity requires the truth; and one's integrity is at stake to allow self-doubt to undermine that truth. To allow others' judgments to become a part of one's self-image, especially when those judgments are untrue, compromises one's power and integrity, because nothing untrue is to be held within when one's authenticity and potential are at stake.

Take a moment now to examine what integrity means to you. In what aspects of your life do you have the most integrity? Why? In what aspects of your life do you have the least integrity? Why? How did you learn about integrity? How do you teach it, model it, mentor it? To what extent do you require it in relationships? To what extent do you allow its absence? Why?

Whose Integrity?

Look particularly at the integrity, or lack thereof, in the family that influenced your own values early in life. If their integrity was, or still is, less than you know your own integrity is to be, then know that the strength required of you to withstand that discrepancy is the strength you have within to tap, and thereby express, your own integrity. Perhaps most important, when you look at the integrity of those persons who influenced your self-doubts, it is reasonable to question their judgment. It certainly is reasonable to give no power to their assessments. It is your own integrity, therefore, that must override the self-doubts so that your potential can be released with integrity.

The gifts to be unleashed on this planet will be dedicated toward assisting a vulnerable humanity. To assist in a meaningful, credible manner, your gifts must have a firm foundation. As those gifts are met with others' resistance, denial, judgment, coercion and numerous other powerful counterforces, only the integrity within will enable you to help others . . . and sustain your own path.

In certain situations in your life right now, integrity may be a deciding, determining factor in an action you are to take. Your authentic self may be at stake in such a situation. By attending to this situation with soul guidance (and not ego impulse), you will edge closer to the opportunities assembling on your path.

DAY NUMBER SEVENTEEN

Guidelines:

Tonight, after this day has been fulfilled,

write a letter to your soul acknowledging the

gifts and potential within you that it

has revealed or reinforced to you today.

DAY NUMBER EIGHTEEN

Guidelines:

Testing the integrity of the soul-directed self.

Today is indeed a test. It is a also a reward. And it is a small, though significant foundation for the soul-directed self to emerge.

The importance of this day is multi-faceted. Numerous aspects of the adaptive self have been targeted for transformation, and some have given way already. Some have not, and at this point in the program they realize that unless they make one last try, they too will be swept into the momentum of exchange.

The Vigil

Because these are subtle, subconscious aspects, they will subtly try to reclaim their position by resurrecting a familiar pattern to see if it can possibly take hold. If the ego is not vigilant — if its integrity is not fully engaged — the automatic familiar pattern may make a showing, in thoughts, behaviors, or even in connection with a situation that manifests in an appealing manner.

The test is to Be, unwaveringly, with all of your qualities fully engaged at all times and at all costs. Even if the truth is that you are vulnerable or insecure, let that be registered. Do not hide or deny it if it is the truth. Truth is most important today, so do not respond or succumb to anything with less than your most courageous, accountable, truthful self.

The reward for this day is that you will find immediately accessible within you the capacity to Be that courageous, accountable, truthful self. You will find that Being is now incorporated into your repertoire, and that it is attracting persons and situations to accommodate, value, respond to and co-create with your Being. What you feel inside, therefore, and the outcomes you create this day can be a powerful verification that what you have exchanged and what you have become can indeed be the loving, loved, creative, authentic self.

So the "test" today is major. Representative remnants of the adaptive self may be pulled together to see if there are enough of them to make a final attempt at remaining active. If they succeed, they will wreak some temporary havoc, sending the ego into the purgatory between the adaptive and authentic. The ego has made such gains that the former pattern will no longer work as masterfully as it once did. But veering into the mere contemplation of such a choice will unhinge the ego from its newly developed repertoire of authenticity . . . and that is a lonely, scary space. The adaptive is no longer functional, so you cannot go back again. But if you abandon the authentic, you lose touch with the security that has developed within, based on your exchanging the adaptive for qualities you know have enduring, positive potential.

The Inauthentic Zone

Since the ego has experienced that security, that value, that self-respect and self-love, they are tangibles now. Hopefully, therefore, when the ego even *thinks* about reviving one of its former patterns, the fear of life in the "inauthentic zone" will bring it back to the truth and security, and it will pass the test.

The ego knows the guidelines for sustaining the progress it has made. However, because it is the Ego, it may have to test the universe by being less than truthful or accountable in order to see what happens. For example, the ego may use the "It will hurt their feelings if I say the truth" routine when it is actually the *ego's* feelings and fear of anger or rejection that summon that pattern back into place. If the ego does momentarily subscribe to such an old tactic — if it does choose to go off the path — the pathway back is always the same: reverse the steps taken to veer away from the truth, integrity, courage, accountability and other qualities to which the ego has been introduced. In fact, the *only* way to return is by invoking these higher qualities.

However, as the distance from the truth increases, the steps to return multiply because each moment of awareness of truth directs the ego to take a step toward it. If the ego resists, that is another incremental step between the ego and truth. Besides, the ego that has been shown truth has been shown it must be acted upon at once. In addition, in exchange for its relationship with truth, that ego has forfeited many of its automatic patterns (doubt, denial, suppressing anger, withdrawing), so that the ego feels the pain of alienation from truth. For the aware ego to venture away from the security of truth anyway is scary; and to do so without those defense mechanisms is, indeed, purgatory.

In that case, the ego is sufficiently aware to see the truth, but it cannot act on it immediately. It has distanced itself from the truth, which it has done many times before, but then it had the filter of denying the truth that was in place. Then it could get by with a lot before the truth cut through again. This time, without that denial in place, the ego sees clearly the twisted compromised situation it is in. It sees the truth, but it is exiled by choice from invoking the truth. Ideally, the alienation and suffering are sufficient for the ego never again to be so compelled.

Because the arena for the ego's consciousness evolution is Life on Earth, difficult situations such as these are inevitable. Ultimately, the ego is evolving beyond the karmic choice of Truth or Consequences. Accordingly, the evolved ego sees by now that the consequences always bring it back to the very truth it had tried to avoid: that consequences are always accompanied with loss of love — either self or others' or both; and that its effort to maintain distance from truth is a constantly insecure and exhausting, ultimately futile, attempt.

The Purpose

For persons designated to create a relationship with truth where none has been before, the assignment *requires* venturing into such difficult settings consciously, specifically for the purpose of retreating immediately by reclaiming the truth and, therefore, registering the how-to's for resolving situations by application of that courage and choice. That is why the ego is likely to venture into this situation at this time: to discover immediately the way back to the soul's unconditional welcoming presence, and to verify the universe's commitment to supporting this effort at authenticity and truth.

Life does not automatically become simple, therefore, with the introduction of this program and these principles; but the guidelines for any situation *are* simple — and constant and consistent. And the path created for following them is filled with extraordinary meaning and purpose.

In some way the experiences of this day will provide a foundation for these dynamic principles to unfold. The day will be an opportunity for the ego either to access the qualities within, and to avert the presence of a pattern assembled to test the ego's resolve. Or, instead of averting, the ego will be lured into the pattern, only to discover it no longer can function there. And ideally, it will not want to.

Either way, this day introduces important dynamics that will define and sustain the soul-directed self.

DAY NUMBER NINETEEN

Guidelines:

Hear and know, here and now, how to Be.

Today there is a sense of relief, of celebration, and it is well-earned. The ego has successfully passed through a familiar, perhaps even tempting, pattern. To do so, the ego accessed the qualities, courage and repertoire newly developed within. As a result, the energies previously allocated to hold that old pattern in place have been reassigned — transformed, literally, to empower the continuation of the new capacities to Be. At this point in this program the lower consciousness patterns have served their purpose. They have perpetuated the consequences of untruth/unlove. They have served to demonstrate to the ego that certain of its choices will inevitably produce the same outcomes. And finally the ego is sufficiently connected with truth so that the soul can reliably substitute a new way of Being each time the ego says no to the former components of the adaptive self.

Trusting The Soul

For this the ego can rejoice. It had known it did not have the capacity to redo all the patterns that contributed to its self-defeating outcomes. On its own, the ego was not even able to *conceive* of a plan that would replace those choices, behaviors, doubts, denials and debilitating emotional grids. Yet much like the tradition of facing the edge of the cliff only to discover that rather than fall, you fly, the ego exhibited a willingness to change — to trust the soul. And as a result, the ego does now know that a plan to replace those patterns exists. The ego also knows how to access that plan, and how to register an alternative to its previous actions. Yesterday's experience assured the ego that it does have the qualities and capacity to hear and follow soul guidance. The ego now knows that *its* assignment is to recognize and resist the presence of limiting, lower consciousness patterns. At that point, the ego has learned, the *soul's* assignment is to immediately assist the ego in adopting a new response, a new repertoire, a new option. And in that glorious moment of soul-directed exchange, the ego can hear and know, here and now, how to Be.

"Here" is the Earth plane, which is only the location. Heretofore it may have seemed that your own ego's challenge was to "Be here." But that is an oxymoron. *Being* simply *is*. It does not adapt to the time, the location, nor the circumstances. Thus, the challenge in reclaiming the *essence* of the authentic self is to focus first upwardly, then inwardly, accessing the soul's guidance each moment and incorporating that into the ego's awareness. Once that is integrated, location and circumstances are to be taken into consideration only as possible parameters . . . *after* Being is registered.

For example, the ego might know it has to be truthful. Yet it might be afraid of hurting someone's feelings. At such a moment the ego is to know the truth and summon the energy to Be — to express that truth. The soul will ensure that the words, tone of voice and timing produce only a positive, healing outcome.

The adaptive self, of necessity, formerly evaluated the circumstances around it and constructed itself accordingly. It focused outwardly, then inwardly; and often only when that scheme faltered did it focus upwardly — usually asking to be rescued by the soul. Now that will change. The universal energies coming into the authentic self (*Be*-ing energies) come from the fourth dimension into the third like a vertical downward column — flowing from *Being* at the top, to *Here* at the bottom, which references the Earth plane third dimension.

Those energies are perfectly allocated from the universe's perspective, and that is what the ego must unconditionally trust. Even though it may feel that in some ways it has lost touch with its former identity and context, the ego must be true to the soul's guidance. The ego must trust that that same context, into which its new identity is merging, can indeed regroup, reorganize, and become a more conscious context, thereby able to accommodate the new self. The authentic self must therefore realize that reclaiming *its* essence creates the opportunity, if not the mandate, for all that is connected with it to do the same. Therefore, any void or loss that appears to result from the ego's positive changes is only an adjustment in relation to those positive changes . . . and ultimately, therefore, only positive. If someone does cease to be in its life, the ego will have developed within whatever it previously needed from that person. The person will have served his/her purpose, and the ego will be stronger as a result of that relationship.

Experiencing The Soul's Love

In other challenges similar to this in the future — of which there will be many — the ego is able to respond with love from within to fill up any space that may be created by such changes. Once the circumstances challenged by the ego's changes realize that the *essential* change is related to creating a greater supply of love through truth, those circumstances will reconvene accordingly. Thus, the ego's automatic response to connect with self/soul love, in the event some aspect of its life does not immediately reorganize to support its new self, is the most important element of reclaiming the essence of the authentic self. That essence *is* love. It always has been love. The adaptive self was not able to hold onto that love, and it suffered as a result. The authentic self is able to reclaim that love and much, much more.

In some situations, however, it may appear that the *reclaimed* authentic self is producing results similar to its first debut — *i.e.*, some persons and circumstances react by distancing themselves. Rather than chase after them because the memory/fear of a resulting void is so terrifying and painful, this time the authentic self accesses the self/soul love that is within . . . and there is no void. In addition, individuals or circumstances are thereby given the opportunity and impetus to change/evolve their reactions based on the love that the authentic self can now powerfully and consistently invoke. Therefore, any one, or any thing, that is prepared to function from its own authenticity will respond to this co-creative opportunity to do so. It only needs to feel the presence of love.

That person or situation may have recoiled as a first response to change (from the adaptive to the authentic) because its first association with such change was to anticipate abandonment; and distancing was its own adaptive mechanism. However, each such person or situation is a part of the larger plan for evolving consciousness and creating more love on this planet. That individual's consciousness, and that situation's consciousness, are being universally directed to forego old, automatic reactions. They are challenged instead to assess the possibility that love, rather than abandonment, will result.

Here again, soul guidance and courage, combined with truth, make the difference. The truth is that this is not abandonment. As the adaptive self exchanges for the authentic, in that "moment" of exchange, the self is, admittedly, focused upwardly and inwardly. The components of its "outward" world may feel abandoned or insecure since they have been constantly created by the adaptive self's outward focus. When it "drops" them, only the truth of the purpose of this extraordinary development — its role in the evolution of truth and love — can hold them in place. Otherwise they would react and move on in accordance with their own patterns and consciousness. Under the universe's guidance, however, they linger. They may retreat, but they do not disappear. They are momentarily held in place, at a distance, unaware that they are awaiting the presence of love to return as it emanates from the radiance of the authentic self.

The love the authentic self returns with is admittedly somewhat different. Perhaps even a lot different if it returns with love whereas its previous connection was needs. But either way, the changes instituted have no consequences. Any "loss" will result in self/soul love being activated within, taking the place of whatever the ego once tried to get from the outside world. Now that love is inside forever. There is no loss to the authentic self. Much more self/soul love has been created, which more than takes the place of some one or some thing not able to respond to the love within the authentic self.

DAY NUMBER TWENTY

Guidelines:

Be and Become only that which you love.

Because there is only one of you in all time, the expression of you is unique — it is divine — it is essential to this planet's, and this humanity's, survival. And if you block it, it will never exist through any other medium. It will be lost, and the world will not have it. Were this to happen, a link in a vital chain would be missing. An ego would have had the will and power to override and sabotage a soul's destiny. Such a provision does not exist in the divine plan.

— Adapted from a Martha Graham letter

At this time in the evolution of human consciousness, the ego's will and power have created enough crises and amassed enough consequences. Your soul's destiny will not be a casualty of those crises — it will be a triumph of inspiration, assisted by an ego willing, not willed — an ego willing to Be, with soul guidance. Therefore, too much is at stake for you to fail at Being. That cannot and will not happen because the universal energies directed to and through you have been assembled carefully, adequately, purposefully to accomplish the re-emergence and sustenance of your authentic self . . . through Being.

Through your Being you are creating a critical mass. It may feel to your ego that you are alone, but your soul rejoices in the communication with other souls whose egos are valiantly taking on this task. And, the more your ego tunes its vibration to its new Being, the more it will connect with its co-creating partners in this joint venture of merging ego and soul consciousness.

Loving Being

The critical mass assembling on the planet is designed to touch and inspire every aspect of your life. The radiant energies of your Being activate the Being potential in others, and others' essence likewise reaches you. How you love, how you express love, how you Be love . . . how you be loving, especially to yourself, is the cue others are seeking. Loving Being, in other words, as well as being loving. Those are the perfect expression of the soul-directed self, and by now, in your own life, your own soul has laid the groundwork for you to Be and Become only that which you love. You can love what you are doing so long as you love how you are Being, and *who* you are Being.

If, therefore, the situation in which you are *doing* (*e.g.*, a job) does not allow or appreciate the essence of your Being, identify the potential you have not yet released there . . . because once you have created the opportunity to unleash that potential, your purpose there will have been fulfilled and you can be released. If the key to identifying that potential/purpose eludes you, know that because it involves Being, it may be more subtle than you are aware. Focus, therefore, not on how to be something different in that job situation. Focus on Being, fully, in *all* aspects of your life and your potential at work will expand.

For example, know that the radius of the energy of your Being extends into and activates the potential within every transaction, as well as activating the potential within other persons. As a result, if you are aware, you can experience an immediate reward for the quality of your Being. You can be joyfully nourished — even exhilarated — by the activation processes your Being catalyzes. (To enhance your experience of Being in your place of work, reflect on the "Organizational Wellness Indicators," on page 122.)

Beaming Being

Consider how this applies to something mundane like going to the grocery store. In the selection procedure for each item you can become aware of which item is at the perfect level of consciousness for you. Instead of non-consciously selecting a container of carrot juice, do so with love. Take time to look at all the containers of carrot juice and sense the energy of the one that is perfect for your home. It is there. Its "being" is beaming out to you. By selecting it consciously, placing it in the basket thankfully, placing it consciously in the refrigerator and tuning into its nutritious energy as you drink it, you are Being with it vs. consuming it. Being with, or in relationship to, all things — animate or inanimate — expands your own Being.

. . . especially in very complex matters such as money. Since its consciousness has been particularly exploited and abused, that eventually will lead to its being replaced. For now, however, in connection with reclaiming the essence of the authentic self, the consciousness of money has a role. Starting with the handling of money, its consciousness responds to the universal principles of order and accountability. Bills that are kept in one's wallet are to be arranged in order: 20's, 10's, 5's, 1's. The faces all lined in the same direction. Coins are not to be randomly strewn in drawers, on the top of the dresser, in the glove compartment, in the bottom of purses or briefcases, or even in a container that never gets emptied.

Money has a value. Treating it non-consciously is a reflection of some aspect within yourself that is not constantly, lovingly, appreciating and relating to everything of value within you. To expand and express your potential fully, however, *all* of the value within you must be consciously incorporated. To become more conscious of your relationship with money — which has a value — will enable the consciousness of your money to communicate back to you aspects of yourself you are not relating to in their full value.

In other words, in the carrot juice and money examples, the principle is that by fully acknowledging and embracing the potential and consciousness — the "being" — of some thing, our Being activates the other's being, and the purpose it can serve in our life is expanded. Not only can it perform the function it is created to serve, such as carrot juice nourishing the body. Its energy can also impact our own energy field and consciousness and expand our own potential . . . and Being.

In your own life and Being, therefore, it is important to allow these kinds of benefits to amplify the changes you will undergo. By attuning your awareness to these expanded possibilities, you will discover meaningful, joyful rewards even as certain other conditions in your life may be slow to respond to your authentic self.

There is much greater reward for your Being to experience. The universe has ensured those rewards. Until many more soul-directed egos appear in your presence — a development which will commence very soon — the universe has arranged for your Being to rejoice in connecting with the essence and potential that resides outside the ego realm. Enjoy, therefore, the potential that your Being awakens and attracts. Seek out the fullest consciousness and "being" in every moment, within every thing, and fully embrace it with *your* new Being.

DAY NUMBER TWENTY-ONE

Guidelines:

Reclaiming the essence of the authentic self.

The essence of your authentic self was divinely created, and through your soul it is present on Earth. That presence is activated only through the ego, however, whose purpose is expressed in loving and whose potential is expressed in Being. Long before this lifetime commenced, your soul was a vibration in the Age of Aquarius, a consciousness into which the human ego is gradually advancing; a consciousness wherein Loving and Being are the only ego experience.

The Cosmic Call

When the call from the cosmos rang throughout this universe, heralding the crisis in consciousness on planet Earth, your soul responded, willing to bring its essence and Loving Being onto the Earth plane experience to create an alternative to ego dominion. Your ego was thereby created in perfect union with conditions on Earth. Arriving in its essence and authenticity, it gradually adapted to Earth plane conditions, struggling eventually for love, for truth and for the meaning and purpose etched in its consciousness but absent from its experiences.

Facing early life challenges in typical human form, your ego adapted its sensitive, loving essence in order to endure insensitive, unloving conditions. Finding no opportunity to reflect its purpose, and little value for its potential, your ego created itself in a variety of ways, seeking the love and recognition that the ego level of human consciousness purposefully seeks.

Throughout the years of registering its Earth experience, your ego ventured in and out of love, in and out of truth, and in and out of touch with its authenticity which, divinely, endured within, despite experiences, actions and feelings to the contrary.

Now, on the Earth plane, another call is sounded. This time to the ego, the level of consciousness that is in crisis. And the first respondents to that call are those from the Aquarian consciousness . . . those whose capacity to Be, and capacity to Love, are essential to the next (quantum) evolution in consciousness: the merger of ego and soul consciousness. Only with that fusion of universal directive will the human ego access the guidance, and be entrusted to steward the resources, the universe has reserved in the fourth dimension to save the future.

The creative gifts and potential within you are essential to that mission. They may have gone unnoticed and unrewarded in the past, but as your courage to Be ignites, so will your extraordinary creativity.

Accordingly, Being — which is fourth dimensional — is the human condition which will attract the guidance and resources. And Being is the Aquarian consciousness your soul and ego are now free to express . . . without consequences.

The karmic system is ending. Truth *or* consequences is the karmic model. Truth and Being are the Aquarian consciousness, which is now assigned to Be on Earth with sufficient power and courage to dissolve the patterns and conditions that perpetuate consequences.

The Aquarian Agent's™ Task

This quality of Being has never been registered on Earth. Thus, the task of the Aquarian Agents™ is extraordinary. They must register their Being at the ego level — both because that is the "how to be on Earth" level, and it also is the precise level of consciousness targeted for transformation. As a result, the Aquarian Agent's™ ego is unique. It has adopted dense, unproductive patterns typical of those creating the crisis in consciousness; but it has also always had in its consciousness an element of truth related to the purpose of those patterns . . . and the truth of its potential to Be, completely free of them.

In this program, that truth is unleashed through the vortex of energies created to exchange the adaptive self for the authentic self. That exchange is both a consciousness experience as well as a mundane one. It creates new awareness and courage. It then directs those qualities back into the mundane situations that have been prepared to evolve their consciousness as well, by responding to the new challenge of truth and authenticity.

When this program's interactive dynamics cease, that vortex continues. Its enduring purpose is to perpetuate the presence and potential of Being and Loving: Being without consequences, and Loving without need for anything other than truth.

Ultimately, when the work signified in this program is complete, humanity's vibration will be embraced by the Aquarian consciousness. Being and Loving will comprise the totality and essence of each moment, and the human ego's capacity to create will have surpassed the destruction left in its wake.

As you and your ego continue the Earth work, the love within and around you will expand as the truth within and around you expands. Your greatest gift is your courage to express the truth. Your highest purpose is to Be according to that truth. And your greatest potential is to experience and express the love that only Being in the truth can create.

Yours is an exceptional life, administered by a devoted soul and an ego with extraordinary willingness to serve. From the universal consciousness that created this all, you are eternally loved and blessed.

Because there is only one of you in all time,

the expression of you is unique. It is divine.

It is essential to this planet's and this humanity's survival.

And if you block it, it will never exist

through any other medium.

It will be lost,

and the world will not have it.

Were this to happen,

a link in a vital chain would be missing.

An ego would have had the will and power

to override and sabotage

a soul's destiny.

Such a provision does not exist

in the divine plan.

Adapted from a
Martha Graham letter

COMPLEMENTARY
EXERCISES

EXAMINING MY RELATIONSHIP
WITH MYSELF

On a separate sheet of paper, rank on a scale of 1 = low to 10 = high.

1. Overall to what extent am I satisfied with myself? ___

2. Specifically:

___ Ego
___ Personality
___ Appearance
___ Wardrobe
___ Health
___ Body
___ Energy
___ Diet
___ Inner strength
___ Honesty
___ Education
___ Intellect
___ Values
___ Sexuality
___ Emotions
___ Spirituality
___ Pets
___ Income
___ Debt
___ Savings
___ Standard of Living

___ Home
___ Automobile
___ Possessions
___ Needs
___ Goals
___ Maturity
___ Security
___ Adequacy
___ Confidence
___ Other (to be filled in)

3. To what extent am I satisfied with my close relationships: ___

Specifically:

___ Mother
___ Father
___ Stepmother
___ Stepfather
___ Children
___ Stepchildren
___ Siblings
___ Grandparents
___ Spouse
___ In-laws
___ Former spouse
___ Former in-laws
___ Lover/s
___ Former lover/s
___ Male friends
___ Female friends
___ Colleagues
___ Spouse's friends
___ Spouse's co-workers
___ College friends
___ Childhood friends
___ Business associates
___ Former business associates
___ Neighbors
___ Landlord
___ Other (to be filled in)

4. To what extent does my life meet my needs? ___

5. In what areas does my life meet/not meet my needs?

6. In what relationships am I not being honest?

7. In what relationships am I giving up my power?

8. What changes or assistance do I need in these areas?

DEBT AS A SPIRITUAL TEACHER:
LACK AS A SPIRITUAL LESSON

A Soul-Based Transformational Ritual

Introduction

Unlike some exercises designed to ease the restrictive conditions on Planet Earth, this ritual asks that before invoking its dynamics, you spend some thoughtful moments reflecting on the relationship between you and your soul.

The reason for this reflection is that you will soon be asking for your soul's assistance in transforming your financial circumstances. You will therefore be asked to connect with your soul so that its power, wisdom and guidance can lead you from the restrictions you have endured and which you now have the opportunity to transform.

Know that your soul has compassionately watched over your struggle with money. Know that it is eager to help release you from the bondage of debt, or whatever you are lacking in your life, so that your energies can be free to do what you came here to do. Most important is your soul's *capability* to free you from this condition. That capability is truly unlimited. So long as you follow the guidelines that lead you along the path your soul creates for you, it will provide the resources for this release.

Because this ritual will transform the energy of the restrictive condition into insight and awareness, you must be willing to acknowledge and, with your soul's guidance, act on that information. Accordingly, your ego's inclination to impose denial or doubt must be recognized and overcome, because your soul has access to energies beyond your ego's grasp or awareness. Your soul is capable of bringing those energies into your life. If your ego resists the soul-directed insights with doubt or denial, your soul will not be able to help. This ritual relies on the insights to create the passageway through which the soul delivers the energies to transform the debt, or lack of it.

Transformation is the key word, and it is dramatically different from change. When a restrictive subconscious pattern is in play, such as financial limitation, the ego finds itself changing situations as a result of the pattern. But, each situation only illuminates a different aspect of the pattern. Until the pattern has been completely illuminated, it must continue to co-create incidents that serve to teach the ego the consequences of perpetuating the pattern. In the mean time, truth is the vehicle through until illumination occurs.

When the pattern is offered the opportunity to transform, it must voluntarily present all of itself for illumination . . . and the ego must be willing to acknowledge the illuminated contents of that pattern, including the truth of its thoughts, actions, needs, feelings, fantasies, denials and whatever else the soul might reveal.

The courage to do so — the willingness to acknowledge the truth — is the aspect of the ego the soul can work with in order to transform the pattern of restriction. With the ego willing to see and act on the truth, the subconscious pattern has no reason nor room to continue. Indeed, the pattern's only function has been to operate in place of the truth. From its onset it had been created with the energy of truth denied. The ultimate purpose of that subconscious pattern, therefore, was to create situations to lead the ego back to that truth.

With the ego fully connected to the soul, through truth, the soul is able to disburse energies not previously receivable by the ego when it was closing down its soul connection through denial, doubt or fear. (The exercise on page 108, "Questions Related to My Relationship With Money," will be helpful in bringing to awareness the dynamics related to your debt or lack.) As you commence this ritual, therefore, be prepared to access the truth of your condition so that your soul can release to you the energies to transform it.

The Ritual

For you to participate fully, and benefit maximally from this ritual, commence the following activities with a commitment to following your soul's guidance for understanding and transforming the patterns that have restricted your relationship with money.

1. On the 15th day of the month, assemble the following: a green candle, a penny, a small amount of mustard, a bakery roll. If you want to add power, obtain a stem of dried eucalyptus from a florist, hobby store, Pier One, etc.

2. On the 15th, write a letter to your soul asking its assistance in transforming your debt into balance and, ultimately, abundance. If your issue is not with debt, but relates to your gifts and creativity not being financially rewarded, ask your soul's assistance in reversing that condition. In either case, write whatever freely and spontaneously comes to you. Avoid editing or judging your writing.

Allow the contents of the letter to pour forth powerfully and truthfully. Your soul will then be able to fill up the space in your consciousness that was emptied through this letter, enabling you to obtain insights related to both the patterns that occasioned the debt (or lack) and the steps you can take to reverse it.

3. After writing the letter to your soul, make a hole in the bakery roll large enough for the candle to fit into. If you have eucalyptus, put a leaf of it in the roll first. Then place the penny into the hole. On top of the penny put a small piece of paper upon which you have written your name, or the name in which the debt (or lack) has been incurred. On top of the paper put some mustard. Then put the candle on top of the mustard.

4. As you prepare to light the candle and transform the energy of the letter to your soul into flame and ashes, commune with your soul as described above. With that soul communication and consciousness, as you ignite the candle and then the letter, focus your conscious mind on committing to follow your soul's guidance. As you watch the energy of fire consume and transform the energy of your letter, know that the fire signifies your soul's ability to assist and guide you in transforming the energy of your debt (or lack). Let the candle burn for as long as your are led, spending at least a few moments after burning the letter quietly reflecting on the meaning of this ritual.

Reflect also on the history of the debt (or lack), knowing that it represents the love you have lived without, and the inner power you have given up, trying to create security and fulfillment in a life wherein only love, not money or possessions or status, can bring you what you really need. Allow the insights and truths you have experienced as a result of the debt (or lack) to surface in your conscious mind and remain there. As your soul's guidance for transforming your condition begins to emerge in your consciousness, know that you must trust and follow that guidance in order to eliminate, and never again allow, the patterns that have occasioned the debt (or lack).

Know also that the first soul-directed steps may not be related to money matters. If you have already pared your expenses and curbed your spending habits, your next step may be to release blocked emotions such as anger, fear and sadness. You might also be challenged to release certain fantasies of others' help, or value for you. You may review the disappointments that such dependency has produced in the past and begin to want to rely only on your own gifts and courage to bring you out of your current condition.

5. After the ritual is completed, take the roll, candle, ashes, etc., and bury them in the earth — or cover them with rocks or leaves. As you do so, say aloud in a powerful commitment to your soul and your self: "I (say your name) release the patterns that have created this debt (or lack) in the name of ___, and I will follow my soul's guidance for transforming it."

6. If not immediately, then soon you will sense the presence of your soul. You are likely to feel gratitude to your soul for providing this reversal in your life. When you feel that gratitude, express it . . . and express freely any other emotions that may be released in this powerful, purposeful exercise.

QUESTIONS RELATED TO
MY RELATIONSHIP WITH MONEY

On a separate sheet of paper, rank on a scale of 1 = low to 10 = high.

1. Overall, to what extent am I satisfied with my relationship with money? ____

2. Specifically:

____ Annual Income
____ Income Consistency
____ Income Increases
____ Savings Accounts
____ Pension
____ Retirement
____ Life Insurance
____ Securities
____ Investments
____ Home Equity
____ Other Equity
____ Debt-free Assets
____ Checking Account
____ Cash On Hand
____ Loans To Others
____ Other (please specify) _____

3. Additionally:

____ Home Mortgage
____ Home Equity Loan

___ Auto Loan/s
___ Personal Loans
___ Credit Lines
___ Finance Company
___ Bank Cards
___ Other Charge Cards
___ Business Loans
___ Education Loans
___ Investment Mortgage
___ Commercial Loans
___ IRS: Taxes Due
___ Medical Bills
___ Child Support
___ Alimony
___ Other (please specify) _____

4. Do I feel secure with my potential to earn money?

5. Am I financially in balance?

6. Does my income meet my needs?

7. Does my savings balance meet my needs?

8. Do my buying habits conform to my financial condition?

9. Do I pay my bills in full each month?

10. Do I pay my bills on time each month?

11. Do I compute my checking and savings balance after each transaction?

12. Do I balance my statements each month?

13. Are my receipts and records kept in order?

14. Am I honest about being undercharged for an item?

15. Am I powerful when returning something I have purchased?

16. Am I organized and timely in filing income tax returns?

17. Am I honest when filing income tax returns?

18. Am I honest in my business dealings?

19. What changes or assistance do I need to improve my financial condition?

20. In what ways am I prepared to make those changes and seek that assistance?

21. In what ways am I not prepared to do so?

22. What can I do to improve my financial condition?

QUESTIONS RELATED TO
MY RELATIONSHIP WITH LOVE

On a separate sheet of paper, rank on a scale of 1 = low to 10 = high.

1. Overall, to what extent am I satisfied with the love in my life: ___

A. Specifically the love I feel from:

___ Spouse
___ Children
___ Mother
___ Father
___ Stepmother
___ Stepfather
___ Stepchildren
___ Siblings
___ Grandparents
___ Lover/s
___ Friends
___ Others in Family
___ Others

B. And the love I feel for:

___ Self
___ Spouse
___ Children
___ Siblings
___ Grandparents

___ Lover/s
___ Friends
___ Others in Family
___ Mother
___ Father
___ Stepmother
___ Stepfather
___ Stepchildren

2. To what extent is this the most love I have ever had in my life? ___

3. To what extent is the love in these relationships increasing ... and if not, why?

___ Self
___ Spouse
___ Children
___ Mother
___ Father
___ Stepmother
___ Stepfather
___ Stepchildren
___ Siblings
___ Grandparents
___ Lover/s
___ Friends
___ Others in Family

4. To what extent am I allowing my dependency to affect love in these relationships ...
    and how can I change that?

___ Self
___ Spouse
___ Children
___ Mother
___ Father
___ Stepmother
___ Stepfather
___ Stepchildren
___ Siblings
___ Grandparents
___ Lover/s
___ Friends
___ Others in Family

5. To what extent am I allowing my anger to affect love in these relationships:

___ Self
___ Spouse
___ Children
___ Mother
___ Father
___ Stepmother
___ Stepfather
___ Stepchildren
___ Siblings
___ Grandparents
___ Lover/s
___ Friends
___ Others in Family

6. To what extent am I allowing my fear to affect love in these relationship:

___ Self
___ Spouse
___ Children
___ Mother
___ Father
___ Stepmother
___ Stepfather
___ Stepchildren
___ Siblings
___ Grandparents
___ Lover/s
___ Friends
___ Others in Family

7. What changes or assistance do I need to improve the quality and quantity of love in my life?

QUESTIONS RELATED TO
MY WORK ENVIRONMENT

On a separate sheet of paper, rank on a scale of 1 = low to 10 = high.

1. Overall, to what extent am I satisfied with my work? ___

2. Specifically:

___ Compensation
___ Responsibilities
___ Meaningfulness
___ Benefits
___ Authority Figures
___ Challenge
___ Job Security
___ Immediate Supervisor
___ Co-workers

3. Additionally:

___ Corporate Values
___ Corporate Policies
___ Policies/Procedures
___ Management Style
___ Hiring Procedures
___ Firing Procedures
___ Raises
___ Promotions
___ Training

___ Morale
___ Turnover
___ Competency
___ Office Hours
___ Smoking/Non
___ Parking
___ Security
___ Lunchtime
___ Expense Accounts

4. Extent to which I am satisfied with my work environment:

___ Location
___ Commute
___ Office Decor
___ Floor Plan
___ Equipment
___ Furnishings
___ Supplies
___ Rest rooms
___ My work area

5. Extent to which I am satisfied with myself at work:

___ Quality of performance
___ Effectiveness
___ My management style
___ Time management
___ Meet deadlines
___ Return phone calls
___ Number of hours work
___ Desk organized
___ Accurate records
___ Competency
___ Values
___ Ethics/Integrity
___ Follow-through
___ Attitude
___ Appearance
___ Attendance
___ Punctuality
___ Emotional maturity
___ Delegating
___ Organization

___ Communication
___ Confidentiality
___ Relations with co-workers
___ Attention to detail
___ Files kept in order
___ Reliability
___ Sexuality

6. To what extent are my business and personal life in balance?

7. To what extent does my work meet my needs?

8. In what areas does my work not meet my needs?

9. What changes or assistance do I need to ensure that my work does meet my needs?

QUESTIONS RELATED TO
MY HOME ENVIRONMENT

On a separate sheet of paper, rank on a scale of 1 = low to 10 = high.

1. Overall, to what extent am I satisfied with my home? ___

2. Specifically:

___ Location
___ Neighborhood
___ Appearance
___ Cooling
___ Heating
___ Security
___ Monthly Payment
___ Upkeep
___ Construction

3. To what extent am I satisfied with its interior:

___ Size
___ Colors
___ Furnishings
___ Floor Plan
___ Lighting
___ Bathroom/s
___ Kitchen
___ Office
___ Library

___ Garage
___ Den/Rec Room
___ Bedroom/s
___ Basement
___ Attic
___ Living Area

4.   To what extent do I enjoy returning home each day? ___

5.   To what extent do I enjoy:

___ Relaxing when I am at home
___ Being there on weekends
___ Inviting others to my home
___ Repairing my home
___ Cleaning my home
___ Working in my yard

6.   To what extent do I regularly:

___ Clean my home
___ Organize drawers, closets, storage areas
___ Repair what is broken
___ Replace what is worn out
___ Eliminate clutter and accumulation
___ Throw away, give away or discard what is unneeded
___ Throw away, give away or discard what is unusable

7.   To what extent is my home environment in balance?

8.   To what extent does my home environment meet my needs?

9.   In what areas does it not meet my needs?

10. What changes or assistance do I need to ensure that my home does meet my needs?

11. The way I will make those changes is:

INVENTORY OF NEEDS

Use the following questions to explore your relationship needs and capacities. If you are involved in or exploring a relationship with someone, ask that person to do the same inventory so that you both can benefit from the insight these topics evoke. You may do these on a separate sheet of paper.

Part One: Examining Myself In A Relationship

1. The qualities I have to offer this relationship are:
2. The insecurities, inadequacies or doubts I have about myself in connection with this relationship are:
3. The qualities I see within the other person that are attractive to me are:
4. The insecurities or inadequacies I see within the other person, and the doubts I have about this person are:
5. The reason I feel this relationship can be fulfilling for me is that:
6. The changes I want to make within myself to enhance this relationship are:
7. The changes I want to make in this relationship to make it more fulfilling for me are:
8. The aspects of this relationship that are essential to me in order for it to last are:
9. The dynamics that would cause me to have to terminate this relationship are:
10. Based on what I know at this point, this relationship is likely to succeed/fail because:

Part Two: Ranking Needs

On a separate sheet of paper, rank on a scale of 1 = low to 10 = high.

____ Truth
____ Integrity
____ Law-abiding

___ Religious
___ Educated
___ Intelligent
___ Patient
___ Non-judgmental
___ Shared values
___ Sexually compatible
___ Touching/being touched
___ Time management
___ Open communication
___ Sensitivity
___ Emotional availability
___ Good listener
___ Flexible
___ Emotionally mature
___ Sense of humor
___ Physically fit
___ Outgoing
___ Quiet
___ Financially secure
___ Attractive
___ Money management
___ Going to movies
___ Watching TV
___ Renting videos
___ Listening to music
___ Participating in sports
___ Attending sports events
___ Going to concerts, plays, etc.
___ Dancing
___ Eating out
___ Cooking at home
___ Reading
___ Meditating
___ Traveling
___ Health consciousness
___ Personal hygiene
___ Environmental consciousness
___ Vegetarian
___ Civic/Community/Volunteer work
___ Contributing to charities, non-profits, etc.
___ Exercise/fitness
___ Drugs: recreational/prescription/over-the-counter
___ Drinking alcohol/caffeine

___ Not drinking alcohol/caffeine
___ Subscribing to allopathic medicine
___ Subscribing to alternative healing
___ Attending seminars, classes, etc.
___ Talking on phone
___ Socializing with business associates
___ Visiting at friends' homes
___ Friends visiting us
___ Visiting family
___ Your liking my family
___ Your liking my children
___ Your liking my friends
___ My friends liking you
___ My family liking you
___ My business associates liking you
___ My children liking you
___ My former spouses/lovers liking you
___ Living together
___ Living separately
___ Sharing expenses
___ Sharing responsibilities
___ Exclusive/monogamous commitment
___ Clutter/cleanliness compatibility
___ Keeping your word
___ Expressing your feelings
___ Expressing your likes/dislikes
___ Accepting me the way I am
___ Helping me make changes
___ Liking the way I look
___ Liking the way I dress
___ Liking my home environment
___ Your trusting my judgment
___ Your trusting my interactions with persons of the opposite gender
___ Your trusting my interactions with persons of the same gender
___ Your telling me if you are attracted to someone else
___ Your accepting my need to spend time with friends and others
___ Your accepting my needs
___ Other (please specify) _____

ORGANIZATIONAL WELLNESS
INDICATORS

1. The owner/manager is respected, trusted and functions as a member of a team, not a detached authority.

2. Information flows freely and effectively, from the top of the organization chart down, and vice versa.

3. Authority, power and responsibility are consistent with the organization chart.

4. Employees are competent, motivated, well-trained and quality conscious.

5. Individuals keep their word and honor their commitments.

6. Salaries, benefits, expense accounts and raises reflect the company's security and adequacy, not its fears, instability or greed.

7. Problematic egos and attitudes are managed effectively or eliminated before they take a toll on productivity or morale.

8. The efficiency of each employee or department is enhanced by adequate equipment, office supplies, office space and other necessary resources.

9. Paychecks are issued with sincere feelings of thankfulness and appreciation.

10. Offices are neat and uncluttered, the atmosphere is orderly and productive even around deadlines, and temperaments and emotions are managed without stress.

11. Employees look forward to arriving for work, they laugh and experience joy

throughout the day, and they leave for home with a feeling of satisfaction and accomplishment.

12. Employees who find employment elsewhere leave on positive, amicable terms.

13. Ethics, honesty, integrity and fairness are emphasized and manifested throughout the corporation.

14. Corporate values and individual values are compatible and mutually reinforcing.

15. Each individual and department is consciously aligned with the purpose of the organization.

16. Accountability is exemplified at the top of the organization and reinforced throughout it.

17. Each supervisor is a teacher and mentor, constantly training, sharing, challenging and empowering.

18. Meetings are started on time, ended as scheduled, and are productive for each person attending.

19. Sales quotas and other profit incentives are based on the corporation's capacity to compete, not on individual fears or drive, unrealistic expectations or needs.

20. Balance is maintained in the time and energy employees devote to business and their personal lives, ensuring that each complements the other, and neither is emphasized at the other's expense.

21. A genuine atmosphere of caring is evidenced. The organization cares about its product or service; it cares about its customers, clients or constituency; it cares about its employees, and they about it; and together they contribute to their community, their state, their nation and their planetary home.

INTRODUCTION: CREATIVE EXERCISES
FOR ENGAGING THE SOUL

By Marily Charles

 The Soul has many different qualities. It is the center of creativity. Together with the Creator and our Creative Soul, we can experience the feeling of true joy. Joy is the emotion at the core of our Being. The Soul is playful, loves all forms of art, is magical and mysterious. The Soul enjoys being nurtured and having fun. It also has a sense of balance, so it will use both the right and left sides of the brain. The following exercises engage the right side of the brain (inner artist) enabling you to learn more about yourself through drawing, music and different forms of writing. Remember throughout these exercise that there is no right or wrong way. Let them just BE. After each Creative Exercise, give yourself thanks for the gift you have given yourself.

Before proceeding with an activity, read all the instructions completely.

Creative Exercise One:
Creating a Sacred Space

1. Choose a quiet spot in your home or yard or garden; perhaps a corner near a sunny window with potted plants nearby.
2. This is your area for you and your Creative Soul. It is a place of reverence and safety.
3. Collect in this space items that are meaningful to you and your Soul: candles, quotes, Angel Cards, incense, shells, rocks, leaves, small pictures or photos. Whatever you choose will bring the energy and vibration you need.
4. Be grateful for this IKUMBA (African word for private and quiet area) which allows you the peacefulness and energy to Be with your Creative Soul.

Creative Exercise Two:
Emotions Drawn on Paper

Invite a few friends to join you in doing this exercise.

1. Give yourself 45 minutes of undisturbed quiet time.
2. Divide a sheet of paper into eight sections. Fold it in half, then half again, and half once more.
3. In each section write one of the following states of Being: Joy, Anger, Illness, Loneliness, Depression, Femininity, Masculinity, Peacefulness.
4. Pencil in hand, center yourself and breathe! Prepare to spend 3-5 minutes on each state of Being.
5. Take yourself back to the last time you felt that particular emotion or state. Truly feel it, allowing the feeling to go up and down your arm, through the pencil and onto the paper. Draw with complete awareness.
6. Avoid drawing symbols (*i.e.*, bolts of lightning or little hearts). Draw only lines and shapes, varying the pressure you use when applying the pencil.
7. Work your way through all the states of Being. Give yourself more time if necessary. Remember to breathe.
8. After completing, share the experience with your friends and you may be surprised at how similar your interpretations of each state are.
9. Notice next time you are at an art show that you will be aware of the different states or emotions the artist is portraying to you, the viewer.

Creative Exercise Three:
Connecting Daily with the Soul

A way to spend quiet time each morning.

1. Wake up 15 minutes earlier each day of the week.
2. Materials: notebook and pen.
3. Before listening to the news or switching on the TV (a cup of tea or coffee is permitted), begin to write.
4. Whatever feelings or thoughts come to you, write them down. This writing is not to be re-read or corrected. This is a form of "throwing up" feelings and putting them there on paper — a way of emptying the emotional vessel.
5. You might want to start your writing by giving gratitude to the new day. You may want to clear up some feelings left over from the previous day. Or there may be dreams you want to reflect on. If so, jot them down. Then continue with how you are feeling right now.
6. Write three pages of anything that comes to your mind.
7. There may be some resistance to writing. If you are feeling anger or resistance to this workout with your Soul, then write down "This is a waste of time . . ." or, "I don't

like doing this . . . " You might want to buy a notebook with smaller pages and graduate to a larger one later. Remember, there is no right or wrong way of doing this exercise. The right brain (Creative Soul) and left brain (critical and judgmental side) are having a tug of war. Acknowledge that.

8. Trust yourself and your Soul; the next day will be easier.
9. Repeat this every morning for seven days. If mornings are a difficult time, find another quiet time during the day. Creative Soul will always be there to write with you and hopes that you will continue this practice.

Creative Exercise Four:
Date with your Soul

This is time to nurture your Soul and replenish the vessel.

1. Set aside one hour.
2. This is to be a fun, light-hearted time for you and your Soul only. No taking the dog for a walk or spending an hour in the gym working out. This is Soul time.
3. Ask your Soul what it would like to do that is fun and special. Perhaps lying in the grass, gazing at the night sky, a bubble bath with candles, taking a walk and allowing your mind to empty, going on a bus ride around the city, meditating under a tree, buying an ice cream. Remembering that the Soul is childlike and playful, your soul may be asking you to repeat an experience you and it had as a child.
4. Once you make this date and set time aside, be sure to follow it through. Canceling, postponing or not following through can be very disappointing to the Creative Soul.

Creative Exercise Five:
A Daily Journal that Records How You
Spend Time and Observe Noise

Do you have Soul time?

1. Materials: notebook and pen.
2. Record each evening how your time was spent. How much time was spent being with family, with work, on the phone, watching TV, reading, etc.?
3. Do you notice that any of your activities allow you to avoid facing relationships with a partner, friend, yourself or Soul?
4. Do you automatically turn on the radio or TV when you arrive home or get into your car? Are you conscious about switching on those noise makers? Try having no radio on in the car for a week, or no TV on at home.
5. If you spend hours reading the paper or magazines, review the purpose of these activities. Try to omit reading anything for one or two days. How will you fill the void? And what feelings are you experiencing as you read this?

6. Reading, listening to the radio and watching TV are certainly not bad. For many of us, they are an important part of our work and responsibilities. Like anything we do regularly, though, it is good to take note, review and, if necessary, reorganize our priorities. In this exercise, we are lead to be aware of the purpose these activities serve in our life.

7. There are many things that you might like to do instead of the above. Again, listen to Creative Soul for answers.

Creative Exercise Six:
Listening to Music

1. Select a time when no one else is at home.
2. Pick a CD or tape of any music of your choosing before reading further. Start the music and then proceed with 3-10.
3. Allow as much time as you can, at least 25-35 minutes.
4. Sitting or lying comfortably, turn the music up very loud
5. Do not change the music you have chosen. There is a reason why you chose this particular piece.
6. Listen to the music. Be alert to any resistance you may feel toward the loudness. Drop the wall of resistance around you, breathe, and let the music flow through you.
7. Notice all the instruments being used in the music. Are there words? What is being sung? Do the words apply to you? The Beatles song, ìI want to hold your handî may be your inner child crying for the love and attention it never had. Be creative and let the feelings and insights rise up while you listen.
8. Music is made up of melody and supporting instruments. Which are you? Which instrument can you relate to? What feelings are coming up?
9. After listening, take time to Be with the music. Creative Soul may invite you to dance or be like a bird. Accept the invitation.

Creative Exercise Seven:
Letter from A Child

1. Set aside 30 minutes of quiet time and space.
2. Materials needed: pen and paper.
3. Centering yourself, take yourself back to your childhood. Choose an age that you would like to be. Take 8-10 minutes to do this step.
4. What were the likes and dislikes of that young child? What were the things you liked to do and were good at? Did you have dreams and ideas for when you would be grown up? Are there fears and anger that you recall from the age you have chosen? Has anything else come to your attention during the few minutes of recalling yourself at this age?
5. Are you aware if this is your animus (male) or anima (female) child you are recalling?

Can you tell which aspect of your child is coming into your awareness, wanting to write to you?

6.   As you prepare to write a letter from this child, you may wish to print the letter like a child would, or use your less dominant hand.

7.   When you are ready, write a letter from the child within to the adult self. Remember to address the letter to your inner child and use the appropriate closing.

8.   Save this letter and keep it near your sacred place for reading at a later time.

Creative Exercise Eight:
Drawing "Being" and Mind Mapping

Before starting, carefully read and follow steps 1-5; then after completing 5, read 6-11.

1.   Set aside 30 minutes of quiet time.

2.   Materials: 2 pieces of paper, pencil and/or colored markers, crayons, watercolors, or any media you choose.

3.   You may do an abstract or concrete painting.

4.   Spend time in meditation centering yourself. Begin to feel deep within what it is like to Be.

5.   When you are ready, being to draw Being on the paper. Again, let the Soul do the painting from deep within. Your arm and the tool in your hand are mere conduits for the Creative Soul. Remember to breathe. Finish the drawing and then go on to step 6.

6.   Looking at the picture quickly, give it a name. The first few words that come to mind will be the title. On the drawing, write the title, date and sign your picture.

7.   On a clean sheet of paper, write the title of your painting in the center.

8.   We are now using the left brain and will be exploring word association.

9.   With your painting in view, allow words to come into your mind. Write the words and phrases on the sheet of paper as if they were the spokes of a wheel, extending out from the center. Return to the center each time your thoughts/ideas change direction.

10. Continue to refer to your drawing. Whatever you are ready to know about your Being is in front of you. Remember to breathe.

11. There may be a need for you to write further about one or two of the ìspokes.î Do so. Creative Soul will be honored to spend more time on creativity.

Creative Exercise Nine:
Letter from the Old Wise Soul

Our Beings are full of wisdom and everything we need to know is within.

1.   Allow 20 minutes of quiet time.

2.   Materials: notebook and pen.

3. Centering yourself and feeling at one with the Universe, ask for the old wise Soul within to speak to you. You may choose to ask this of the dream-maker the night before you go to bed.

4. See yourself as a 70-80 year old, or even older. Visualize yourself at this age, writing to the younger you. What do you want to say? What wisdom do you want to pass on? What are the activities that you enjoyed during your life, and want to share? What value changes or insights did you gather along the way. What dreams would you encourage the current you to pursue?

5. Now write the letter. Address and date the letter to yourself on whatever day you have written it.

6. Place the letter in a stamped, self-addressed envelope and ask a friend to mail it to you whenever the letter communicates that it is ready to be sent. We know the Creative Soul will enjoy this letter.

Creative Exercise Ten:
Soul Drawing Soul

A better understanding of someone close to you.

1. Set aside 20-30 minutes of quiet time and space.
2. Materials needed: paper and pencil. Colored markers may be used.
3. On the paper, outline a format 8 x 6.
4. Spend 3-5 minutes centering, focusing, feeling and being with the person you choose to draw.
5. When you are ready, begin to illustrate the insights and feelings that come up from deep within about this person. Draw in the 8 x 6 format outlined on the paper. Remember to breathe.
6. Draw only shapes and lines. (*i.e.*, no symbols like stars or lightning or rainbows.) This is an abstract portrait of the person. Your Soul knows this person very well and will help you to make lines and shapes. Your arm, hand and pencil are the conduits from your Soul to the paper.
7. Upon completion, write 10-15 sentences about your picture and how you are feeling. What insights have you had about this person?
8. Place the drawing in your home where you can view it as you go about your day. Be with the image for a day or two, giving yourself more time to better understand and connect with this person.

Creative Exercise Eleven:
Poem about the Authentic Self

1. Set aside 20 minutes of quiet time and place.
2. Materials: writing paper, pen or pencil, or a computer.

3. Being centered and still, give some thought to what qualities, values or characteristics make up your Authentic Self.
4. Jot these thoughts down as they come.
5. Listening to the Soul, the words will begin to flow onto the paper.
6. Find a sentence that is meaningful to you that you can repeat throughout the poem. For example, "And the river flows on" or "Myself I do trust, I can." These words will be repeated very other sentence or two. Remember to breathe.
7. Taking the qualities you have written down and this main theme sentence, begin to gather the words for the poem.
8. Give the poem a title. Print it on a computer. If you do not have a computer, ask a friend to print your poem. And don't forget to sign it. The Adaptive Self will be amazed by the beauty of your writing.

South African born, Marily Charles has lived in Denver, Colorado for the past 20 years and has studied art and creativity on four continents. Her love of watercolor is evident in her work, and through her art she has learned that the painted picture is beautiful; but it is the bigger picture of life that excites her. With joy and passion, she facilitates, counsels, and teaches workshops encouraging others to reawaken their creativity. The exercises in this section were lovingly compiled by Marily.

For every person we have named,

there are a hundred who speak;

for every hundred who speak,

there are a thousand who know;

for every thousand who know,

there are ten thousand who do not yet know

because their truth lies still deeper than

all the ones who speak and

know and can be named.

And every one of us is needed now.

To do whatever we can do: to be named,

to speak, to know, to not know.

And every one, the one who can be named,

who can speak, who knows,

and who does not yet know,

is within each one of us.

Adapted from
The Feminine Face of God
By Sherry Ruth Anderson and Patricia Hopkins

What I am concerned with

is my readiness to obey

the call of truth,

from God,

from moment to moment,

no matter how inconsistent

it may appear.

My commitment is to truth,

not consistency.

— *Gandhi*

SUPPLEMENTARY
READING

EMOTIONAL INTEGRITY

In the Great Library of Alexandria where Aristotle's writings were displayed, the section on metaphysics denoted the study of humanity's relationship with the soul. Now over a thousand years later, metaphysics as an emerging new age discipline explores the spiritual dimension of humanity's role and purpose in the evolution of consciousness.

In addition, as a guide to daily living, metaphysics teaches that love is humanity's emotional reward for its courage to express the truth, and that the quality and quantity of love in one's life are determined by one's relationship with truth. Accordingly, truth is the word humanity uses to describe the quality of information that comes through the soul to the ego from the universe, the creator, the consciousness frequently referred to as God.

The Matrix of Truth and Ego

Even though the matrix from which truth extends vastly exceeds the parameters of humanity's consciousness, humanity is aware that truth is the mechanism propelling its evolution. Humanity also recognizes that the constancy of truth sustains the contact between creator and human and all that is in between.

How humanity manifests the relationship between truth and love is determined by the ego — the leading level of consciousness through which humanity registers it choices and actions on Earth. Assigned to distinguishing truth despite doubt and deceit, and love in a world spiked with anger and fear, the ego's multiple-choice consciousness struggles to learn the lessons of the many alternatives. Ultimately, the ego selects one of those options from the category of "Truth or Consequences."

From a mundane perspective, because humanity resides in a cause/effect universe, different types of choices produce different results. From a universal perspective, each moment provides humanity with one option which, if chosen, will evolve its consciousness. That option is soul-directed. The soul's source of communication is truth, disbursed to the ego through intuition. Any choices other than truth will result in experiences from which humanity will have to learn. Eventually humanity becomes saturated by learning from experiences and is able to make the choice to learn through enlightenment instead.

Enlightenment reveals the purpose. It is accessed through truth. By understanding the purpose for which something exists rather than encountering it because there is a lesson to learn, humanity is able to derive much greater meaning from its experiences on Earth.

At the instant when the cosmos fuses truth into the ego's awareness, the result is a quality of information and meaning wholly unobtainable by and uncontainable within the logical, rational, inductive or deductive constructs of the human mind.

The Ego and Emotions

Magnificent and awesome as it is, however, the evolution of consciousness facilitated by the experience of truth is not the sole dynamic affecting humanity's activities on Earth. The creative consciousness that sustains truth, evolution and life on Earth has also enriched the human experience with a band of emotional energy. Like a connective tissue, it provides a nurturing, challenging, interactive environment that enables humanity to relate intimately to thoughts and actions that comprise and perpetuate its evolution.

Four types of energy patterns comprise the texture of humanity's emotional plane. As a result, there are four principal emotions from which humanity's emotional repertoire unfurls: love, anger, fear and sadness.

Each of these emotions serves a purpose in humanity's evolution. From a universal perspective, humanity comes to this planet to experience love. From a mundane perspective, humanity is challenged to derive the power from truth and the security from love in order to transform the other contrasting emotions.

Two of those other emotions, anger and fear, are disturbing, disruptive and sometimes destructive. However, they are a purposeful part of the universal plan because energetically they provide a resisting force which challenges love to expand and grow stronger. By multiplying itself to meet their challenge, love ultimately overwhelms and absorbs anger and fear and thereby transforms their energy into love.

Sadness, which is the ego's response to loss of love, is the emotional outcome when unexpressed anger and fear accumulate and block the ego's relationship with love. In that case, each time the ego allows itself to acknowledge and feel the sadness, it can access the message contained in the sadness — a message related to loss of love. In other words, sadness, when expressed, guides the ego back to love.

The Purpose of Emotions

Admitting and releasing anger, fear and sadness in a productive way can be made easier by understanding their purpose as well as the steps that lead to their transformation. Both their purpose and their transformation are related to the ego's experiencing more love.

Love is the enduring emotional energy. Its purpose is to create, sustain and give meaning to life. In so doing, it bonds humanity in family, friendship and mating relationships.

Anger, too, has a purpose: to create change. And the principal change it creates is to challenge love to expand. Because anger is humanity's automatic emotional response when its needs are unmet, the hidden message of anger is, "I need to feel more love." Anger is divinely designed to be purposefully uncomfortable so that humanity does not hold onto it. It is to be released immediately at the moment it is felt because it embodies both the quality and quantity of energy necessary to interact perfectly in the environment and produce the change needed at the moment. Because it is to be a non-enduring emotion, once it has interacted in the environment and created the change —which is to challenge love to expand — it ceases and is replaced by love.

The third emotion, fear, also has a purpose: to alert humanity to situations that are life threatening. And the purpose of sadness is to expand humanity's emotional capacity so that once the sadness is released there is a greater capacity to feel love.

Love

Subjectively, love is the most enjoyable emotion. Ideally, all situations and individuals would be filled with so much love there would be no unmet needs and life would be bliss. That describes the promise of the Age of Aquarius, for which humanity is currently undergoing emotional reconfiguration in preparation to enter.

Until humanity's consciousness evolves to that Age, however, the real world of today is quite different. In it, humanity is still trying to gain mastery over an ego that is too unevolved and untruthful to have earned that quality and consistency of love. In addition, the collective of humanity is jammed in traffic snarls, foiled by computer viruses and hackers, harried by incompetence, held hostage to violence, subjected to lies and disinformation, and facing a future of economic uncertainty.

Anger

In contrast to the smoldering kind of anger that can lie buried within and turn volatile when it comes out, spontaneous anger becomes a signal that it is time to pull back, change situations, examine values and priorities and create alternatives. Indeed, it is difficult not to respond with anger in certain daily life challenges. But it is much better to acknowledge the anger and respond with it than to manipulate it, suppress it, and allow it to build to out-of-control proportions as a result.

If a mantra, relaxation exercise, marathon or massage is consistently adequate to eliminate the energy of anger, the person is truly blessed to be spared the karma of anger. For the majority of the population, and even for the metaphysical community, certain of the demands these days are not being meditated or massaged away. As a result, anger is being suppressed or denied and is taking a toll on the supply of love.

Rage

Anger can be destructive when allowed to store up and be used in excess. Having lost the opportunity to create change, it becomes ammunition for use later. In addition, manipulated, suppressed anger loses the vibration and properties ascribed to anger because it becomes rage.

When an individual habitually suppresses anger instead of releasing it, that energy accumulates in a reservoir within. It then commingles with anger stored up from other occasions and eventually builds up so much tension that it simply must be released . . . inappropriately. A minor event will trigger an uncontrolled outburst, or the anger will be displaced onto the wrong person, or a subtle strain of it will sabotage in a variety of ways: important items misplaced, meetings forgotten, phone calls not returned, broken commitments, lost keys, unread mail, unpaid bills, burned dinner, speeding tickets, accumulated clutter, excessive talking, eating, drinking, drugs, confusion, withdrawal, depression.

Needs

Because anger is a more intense emotion than love (love is more enduring; anger is more intense), if anger is continually held inside instead of being expressed, the needs occasioning it are not being met so the situation or relationship has no chance of succeeding. Since love expands by meeting the challenge of anger, if the anger is not expressed the love in the relationship cannot grow.

Eventually, the build-up of that intense emotion can overwhelm the love. The love may still be underneath. But if the relationship is constantly riddled with anger, the environment is inconsistent, trust erodes and expressing love becomes a risk. After a while there is too much pain and the suppressed love turns into dependency. An angry/dependent relationship may last for years . . . but only because both parties have compromised their need for love and adopted automatic patterns of survival.

Fear

Oddly enough, such a pact can easily produce fear because even inappropriate fears are fueled by the excess of anger that accumulates in a dysfunctional, dependent situation. When fear is activated in its most useful form, it triggers adrenaline and assists humanity's flight from danger. It is unpleasant at the time, but it is appreciated afterwards. Like anger, however, fear can be inappropriate and disturbing if it accumulates.

Fear is designed to last as long as the threat to life lasts. When a person has successfully escaped, or when the danger has abated, the body's alarm systems calm down. If a person lives with fear constantly despite no real, imminent threat — such as unnecessarily anticipating a heart attack, burglary, car accident, loss of job or spouse — then the fear becomes unproductive. Because its presence is not occasioned by a threat which eventually goes away, the longer it lasts the greater its loss of focus. Then the fear generalizes and results in a nonspecific anxiety or, worse, paranoia. The fear-ridden person therefore loses contact with the truth and, as a result, with love.

Anger-Based Fear

In the relationship between fear and anger, when anger builds up and blocks one's relationship with love, a powerful pattern is at work. Anger becomes a constant companion and only others fortified with their own suppressed anger are interested in being around. Individuals with an open love vibration find the below-the-surface anger too abrasive and too unpredictable. They may not come right out and say "Your anger is too uncomfortable for me to be around;" they just disappear or never have time to get together.

Even when someone does come into the life of a person with suppressed anger and fear, although the love seems assured, so long as those volatile, insecure emotions are stored inside, the ecstasy will be short and the disappointment deep because it was needs and not love that felt so strong. Only the capacity for love, not the demand of unmet needs, will have the resilience and stability to sustain a relationship. Unmet needs can attract a person — a person with similar unmet needs, that is. But the needs will soon give way to inadequacy, and each person will return to the needs-based quest.

Because the pattern of accumulating anger continues to insulate a person from love, the fear that sets in is that the anger will keep that person from feeling love. To some extent the fear is unrealistic because one's physical life is not actually endangered. In another way, however, the fear is well-founded because love is essential to a balanced, fulfilling life, and suppressed anger destroys that possibility.

Sadness

Deadly patterns such as these will perpetuate alienation from love and truth until the sadness from being so out of touch with every one and every thing on the planet causes the person to grieve so deeply that the emotional catharsis makes room for recovery. In that instance, the person must first acknowledge the truth of the patterns that perpetuate such inevitable outcomes. Then the person must commit to being honest in relationship in order to attract the love that is needed.

Integrity and Emotions

Only truth has the power to transform the conditions that threaten humanity's emotional security, and only if anger and fear are successfully transformed will there be enough emotional power to restore love.

Emotional Honesty and Courage

In a very real sense, our emotional honesty and courage are our only hope. Despite the stigma attached to being spiritual and admitting to having some anger, the issue is even more than just emotional integrity. It requires us to establish a loving, unconditional model for recognizing and productively releasing these emotions wherever they are. The challenge means being willing to accept that being loving and spiritual does not guarantee that the residue of anger from childhood abuses and abandonment, failed marriages, exploitation in careers and other inadequate situations has disappeared.

The responsibilities of life on this planet at this time can be overwhelming. . . and if our friends are too spiritual to talk about our frustrations, including anger, then either we will take out those frustrations on our children when we do not mean to, or we will stuff them down and go on, knowing they will resurface inappropriately, out of control, as an accident, illness, bounced check, etc.

The value and scope of our work on the planet do not allow us to exempt any aspect of ourselves from any degree of emotional openness and integrity. Consequently, the spiritual community must open its heart to some members who are reluctant to admit their anger, and embarrassed or afraid to ask for help, but whose courage in transforming them will be a gift to the planet, the community and the individual archetype as well.

Likewise, because so many fears are actually unfounded, we need to feel the support, freedom and courage to test the reality of those fears. If it feels like someone has emotionally withdrawn, we must have the courage to ask if that is true. If we fear the significant person in our life is interested in someone else, instead of worrying, we must ask for the truth. Often it brings great relief to test our fears because we find they were unfounded. Besides, if we test the fear and the answer is yes, then the reality has been established and the energy consumed by dreading or wondering can be put to use preparing for the consequences or making new plans.

Transforming Anger into Love

The primary objective for expressing anger and fear is to maintain emotional integrity and thereby retain the power to create an emotional environment filled with enough love to meet everyone's needs. Love is the emotional reward for truth. Therefore, if we are angry and deny that, or suppress the emotion, we are not being honest and we are restricting the continuous creation of love.

By releasing such suppressed emotions, humanity's anger can be transformed. Therefore, some who are willing to serve the universe must be willing and equipped to recognize and help heal the anger and fear on planet Earth. This means providing a sufficiently loving, non-judgmental, tenacious environment for that emotional energy to be expressed and released.

Denial Does Not Help

Not everyone is interested in such a task, obviously. Some people want to deny the existence of anger and fear except in a context totally removed from their lives. Others want to ignore or put off dealing with those emotions. And some want to stay away from others' anger because it reminds them of their own which they are unwilling to admit.

Still others who have finally settled into a lifestyle with love and support are not attracted to the grueling and dueling required to assist someone trying to cope with suppressed anger — or rage. There are others who would say that loving people are not to spend their energy thrashing around in anger. Like oil and water, the two do not mix, they would say, so let the angry people find one another.

That may be valid. But the spiritual community has acknowledged its role and availability in healing the planet. Does it reserve the right to select its tasks? Is the appeal of recycling waste confined to potato peelings and newspapers? Doesn't the human energy wasted by anger qualify, too? Is it just too much to expect to find a way to make anger biodegradable?

Denial Does Not Heal

By avoiding unpopular emotions, and especially by denying them, humanity maintains control over them, thereby limiting the manifest destiny of love which is to expand and fill this universe. Humanity's manipulation of disruptive emotions likewise restricts their being released, despite the fact that they were purposely created to be encountered and absorbed by love so that its presence replaces their own.

In the universal plan that created the emotional plane, neither anger nor fear were to be permanent or enduring. Nor were they to be stored inside individuals to become abundant on the planet. Anger and fear were created only to provide a contrast to love. This is a dual universe. For every action in it there is an equal and opposite one. Anger and fear were designed to function accordingly in relation to love. They are the emotions that challenge love to expand. And if they are denied and stored inside, they build up to the extent that they threaten love instead.

Consciousness and Emotions

Ideally, the characteristics of anger and fear make them so uncomfortable that humanity is both eager and willing to express them and be rid of them. However, because humanity is evolving an ego, subconscious and unconscious at the same time that it is struggling with anger and fear, its subconscious can develop patterns that prevent the release of those emotions. Humanity's unconscious can be even more intractable, refusing access to those emotions and blocking the ego's awareness that they are buried inside.

Then there are the ego's own self-defeating devices obstructing its emotional transformation. It frequently denies its anger, overcompensates for its insecurity, lies to hide its inadequacy and equates its worth with its cars and jewels and money and things.

That the ego needs to feel more love is painfully clear. The emotional deficits on the Earth planet are symbolized by the enormity of the financial debts it hosts. Its individuals have desperately charged and spent and consumed and borrowed in a futile effort to escape their emotional pain. After huge investments and risks and disappointments they have had to discover that love is not for sale and the roadway into materialism detours into a dead end.

Truth

If we simply acknowledge the truth of our anger at the moment we feel it, express it without labeling others or dragging up the past, ask for the change we need and then express our gratitude when our integrity and courage produce more love — especially within — then we can become more honest and direct and release the emotions restricting our love.

If we want to be really brave about it, we can ask others to help us identify our anger. They may even ask us to help them do the same. In any event, when we begin to change the patterns we have co-created by suppressing our emotions, it is advisable to let those around us know that we are no longer going to pretend that some things are okay when they are not.

If, as a result, learning how to express anger includes times when extra anger from the reservoir comes out and is more than the situation deserves, we must admit it at the time. By preparing others for a few miscues until the reservoir inside is cleared out, we will be able to obtain their trust and assistance until the new approach finally starts to work.

I Need To Feel More Love

Since the hidden plea behind anger is, "I need to feel more love," if the expression of anger is insufficient to create the changes in a relationship, then it may be necessary to change relationships. In the movie "Sunday Bloody Sunday," an intense drama involving dependency, jealousy, anger and trust,

Glenda Jackson says, "Something is better than nothing, but nothing is better than some things."

The losses that result from expressing anger are related only to those situations or relationships that inherently lack the capacity to meet our needs. The fact that releasing one's anger has to be the mechanism for being freed from inadequate situations may be lamentable, but it is certainly better than the involuntary bondage of an angry, dependent relationship that gets worse every day.

Even though it is a fact of life on Earth, anger is a controversial energy. Granted, it can be destructive. Many people have experienced it in an unfair, unloving and even abusive way. But not because the anger itself, in its purest form, has those qualities. Only when we hold it inside and manipulates it does anger then manipulate the energy of love.

Releasing Manipulated Emotional Energy

If anger is seething inside it is passively destructive, and if it is released it can at least have a chance to destroy whatever conditions lack the capacity to manifest the quality and quantity of love that one needs. Therefore, if anger has accumulated, it already is creating problems. The ego feels safer with the anger suppressed or denied, but that is because the ego decided to manipulate its environment by pretending the anger did not arise.

Rather than trusting the truth of its emotions, and trusting their purpose, the ego suppressed the anger to get what it wanted. The anger was actually there to help the ego get what it needed, or at least to avoid a situation that appeared to the ego to be able to meet its needs, but which ultimately would turn out otherwise. Trusting anger to guide it to love is indeed a challenge to the ego. But for the ego whose suppressed anger is obstructing love continually, the truth of its anger is the ego's greatest hope.

Because the anger stored inside has had to be manipulated in order even to be there, unless we cease doing that to ourselves we will never experience the power and security that the truth of our emotions can bring . . . and we will not be given the power to change this planet until we can trust the power of truth to change our lives.

MANAGING HOLIDAY STRESS

Although making resolutions usually comes at the end of the holiday season, this year it may be helpful to make the resolutions at the beginning. Spend a few moments, then, contemplating your plans for the upcoming holidays. Answer each of these questions with a *yes* or *no* and take time to become aware of the emotions you experience with each response.

1.   You plan to travel for the holidays even though you prefer to stay home.
2.   You are staying home but wish you could be elsewhere.
3.   You make plans to be with others based on guilt or obligation.
4.   You make up excuses for not being available or for not keeping commitments.
5.   You get depressed during the holidays.
6.   You subject yourself to situations that make you feel inadequate.
7.   You vow not to gain weight but you do.
8.   You drink too much.
9.   You go to parties you do not enjoy.
10. Your life is unfulfilling and the holidays make it feel worse.
11. You create the impression that a relationship is working even though it is not.
12. You are overwhelmed with sadness because of someone who no longer is in your life.
13. You manipulate others to be with you or to meet your needs.
14. You fantasize that the holidays will bring you and your family closer together.
15. You try to please others to gain their love and approval.
16. You encounter anger and arguments that make you feel uncomfortable.
17. You are afraid to express what you really feel.
18. The person you are in a primary relationship with is not welcome where you are spending the holidays . . . or vice versa.
19. You are jealous of attention or affection that others get.

20. You require your children to meet your needs instead of adjusting your plans to meet theirs.
21. You dislike gift-giving but are afraid to say so.
22. You buy gifts you cannot afford.
23. You hope that a special gift will make up for the love you have been unable to express.
24. You equate the cost of a gift with the amount of love being given.
25. You dislike the holiday crowds and commercialism but dutifully shop anyway.
26. You cannot imagine saying you want to exchange love instead of gifts this year.
27. You doubt you have the option to spend the holidays as you would like.

If Your Answers To The Above Are Yes

You can change, and the most powerful time is now. Whenever you become aware of a change you need to make, behind that moment of realization is a reservoir of energy available to sustain the envisioned change. However, if the insight is not acted on, energy from that reservoir is depleted. Eventually, if you refuse to take action on your own, the energy to produce options will cease. Then your life will be rearranged so that the changes happen to you instead of through you.

The holidays become unbearable when you choose to compromise. The alternative is to express what you feel and need and encourage others to do the same. Then the automatic patterns that have been unfulfilling for both sides can be replaced with plans that everyone creates together.

Many people need to experience the freedom to express their truth and to be who they are and to discover that those qualities are lovable and acceptable. The last thing they need is another gift-wrapped item with which to try to fill up the emptiness. This holiday season you can offer an alternative: openness, emotional availability, truth and a demonstration of love that becomes a ray of hope.

You can say to others in a loving way that you need the holidays to be different this year. Tell them what you would like, urge them to say truthfully what they would like, and then let them feel your availability and support in making plans that will work better for everyone involved. By allowing yourself simply to Be, you can demonstrate a quality of self love and offer to others a quality of love that is available not from obligation or manipulation, but from a foundation of values and emotional integrity that you have the courage to express. No greater gift exists either for you or for them.

Amidst such emotional achievements, if you are still unable to renegotiate the gift-giving routine, then suggest buying simple gifts and make special plans for the items you do receive. Give them to churches, synagogues, charities, shelters for the homeless and abused, institutions for the mentally ill and disabled, nursing homes, respite centers . . . to people who genuinely are in need.

The true *spirit* of giving is to do so with joy. If the joy you might feel from giving to a stranger in need is overwhelmed by fear of the reaction of the person who gave you the gift, perhaps you are not quite ready to challenge the tradition. At least, however, you can break the pattern of obligation and on your own, commence preparing for the changes that create a more equitable redistribution of resources on the planet. To begin participating in that process now is both a joyous relief from the past and an inspiring experience of the security of the future.

If Your Answers To The Above Are No

You have managed to avoid or transform a set of values and emotional vices that have a devastating grip on a vast number of people. As a result, you are likely to find that others reveal to you their own frustrations and confusion because they sense you have discovered a solution to holiday distress that they would like to learn.

When this occurs, be prepared to share with others how you found the inner strength to participate in the holidays, in accordance with your beliefs, values and needs.

Know that many people realize the emptiness of the patterns in their lives but do not know another way to be. They are afraid of being rejected or hurting others' feelings, yet they come together under holiday conditions that hurt more people more deeply than the truth could ever allow.

Suggest that they have other options. Assure them that you struggled with similar guilt and fear and that you realize how powerful the patterns from the past can be. Be assured that as you admit the risks and radiate the rewards, the security within your being will convey the most inspiring message of all.

GUIDELINES FOR TRANSFORMING
ANGER TO LOVE

 There are many approaches to resolving anger. These are principles to assist in acknowledging and expressing the anger that has already accumulated, so that its energy can be transformed back into the energy of love.

1. There are four principal emotions: love, anger, fear and sadness. Each of them has a purpose. The fundamental purpose of emotions is that they are to be expressed. They are to enrich humanity's experience of life on Earth. It is an issue of emotional integrity when the human ego hides or denies or manipulates the truth of its emotions.

2. Anger is the emotion that ties humanity to the past.

3. Fear is the emotion that lures humanity away from the present and into the future.

4. Love is the emotion that creates the present.

5. A relationship created with love knows no joy greater than Being with that love in the present.

6. A relationship based on inadequate love escapes the present via anger (dwelling on the past) or fear (fantasizing about the future).

7. Love is the enduring, creative emotion. It is humanity's emotional reward for its courage to express the truth. Accordingly, the quality and quantity of truth in one's life determine the quality and quantity of love. Love is also humanity's

automatic emotional response when its needs are met. While it would be ideal if there were sufficient love on Planet Earth to meet everyone's needs, that is not yet possible because the human ego's relationship with truth is not that constant. Until love does manifest on Earth with such abundance, humanity is given other emotions to challenge and expand its relationship with love.

8. One of the most challenging of those emotions is anger. It is often experienced as an unloving emotion. However, the truth is that anger is not unloving. It is intense, and unpleasant — and it has been targeted for extinction as soon as there is adequate love on this planet for everyone. But in the meantime, rage, not anger, is the unloving emotion.

9. When anger has been manipulated and stored inside rather than being expressed, there is a reservoir of anger built up and available to be tapped inappropriately. That storehouse accumulates into rage, and then anger has lost its integrity. Its energy no longer perfectly matches the situation.

10. Rage is anger that has been manipulated, stored inside, and therefore has the capacity to erupt out of proportion to a situation. Rage is destructive because it is the product of manipulating truth — emotional truth. Rage has accumulated because of numerous occasions when a person did not express anger. As a result, that person pretended something was all right when it was not. The truth was that the person was angry. The rage accumulated because the person was not emotionally truthful.

11. Because of the frequent erroneous association between anger and rage, anger is often perceived as destructive. On its own, anger is not destructive. It is more intense than love, but its intensity does not destroy love. In fact, because love is the enduring emotion, it is possible to be very angry with someone and be very in touch with the love for that person at the same time.

12. Given the many tangled emotional conditions in humanity's experience, the tendency to deny anger is perhaps understandable. However, to be angry and yet act otherwise is both dishonest and manipulative. In addition, such a strategy is not insurance against anger. Rather, it insures that by holding onto the anger by suppressing it, it will be there constantly, eventually turning into rage and becoming the very behavior one was trying to avoid.

13. Anger is a God-given emotion. It is humanity's automatic emotional response when one's needs are not met. Its purpose, therefore, is to create change — to create a change in the quality and quantity of love that is available. The hidden message of anger is, "I need to feel more love." When it is not manipulated, anger is divinely meted out in the perfect quality and quantity to interact in the environment and create the change that is needed.

In so doing, anger challenges the hidden love potential in a relationship or situation.

14. Because anger is a purposefully disruptive energy, it is designed to impact a situation in a manner that disturbs it, reorganizes it, and ideally contributes to unleashing the love that is available but not being expressed. Indeed, anger is often the response to such unavailable withheld love. Regardless of the circumstance, however, to deny one's anger means denying the emotional tool that can be used to help identify which situations can, and which ones cannot, meet one's needs.

15. Individuals who suppress anger are attractive to, and attracted to, others who do the same.

16. When any emotion, including love, is repeatedly suppressed to the extent it is not acknowledged and expressed, a condition sets in. Dependency is the condition that results when the love in a relationship is manipulated, controlled, withheld, or in some way impaired from being active and reinforcing. Often the love is suppressed because anger has not been expressed and the buildup of anger overwhelms the love. In connection with unexpressed anger, depression is a condition that results when anger has not been experienced or expressed.

17. Guilt is a condition that combines anger and fear: anger toward something that occurred in the past, and fear of the possible consequences.

18. When the buildup of anger continually obstructs one's relationship with love, unrealistic fears develop. Whereas the reason humanity has a capacity to feel fear is to signal life-threatening circumstances, when one's relationship with love is threatened, fear can be the response. The fear is that there will not be enough love in the person's life. If unrealistic fears are not expressed, and thereby dispelled, anxiety is the condition that develops . . . and its elevated state, paranoia, can ensue when fear compromise one's access to truth and love.

(Since the holiday season is filled with guilt-based actions, review the "Managing Holiday Stress," on page 143 before you repeat any patterns this program can help you cease.)

19. The most productive way to manage anger is to have enough love inside that love, rather than anger, can be the immediate response to any situation. The most productive way to express anger that love has been unable to absorb is to follow three steps: 1. Acknowledge the anger by saying "I'm feeling angry." 2. Identify what you are angry about. 3. Ask for the change you need. Then, after the anger has been expressed and the change has occurred, finalize the transaction with some expression of love. "Thank you for listening to me" or "I appreciate your willingness to try and change."

20. Once the anger has been expressed, the love feelings will return because love is the enduring emotion. Anger is a purposefully uncomfortable emotion so that one does not find it appealing to hold on to it. So once the feelings of love return, it is important to express them.

21. When disciplining children, this principle is especially important. A parent may be angry with a little child and react by saying ,"You cannot go outside the rest of the day." The child goes to her room and in a few minutes the parent hears the sobs and feels regret, realizing, "I was too harsh." At that moment, when the love returns, it is important to express the love — go to the child and comfort her. The anger has done all it can do. Love has returned. That is the emotion to be expressed as soon as it returns. Acting on that emotion at that time may produce a renegotiated disciplinary action. It will surely produce a better outcome than alienation.

22. Unfortunately, many individuals experienced anger as an unloving emotion when they were children; but that unloving, punitive, judgmental emotion was rage. Nevertheless, if they determined that they never wanted to behave that way themselves, or concluded that all anger had those unloving properties, then understandably they would be reluctant to show their own anger.

There are no ordinary moments . . .

in every moment,

the quality of your life is on the line.

— *Dan Millman*

LOVING BEING

To be registering a model for Being does necessarily include registering a model for loving, which model derives its principal initiative from the state of loving to Be — or, loving Being — or, having a loving response to Being.

To love Being is to love constantly if one has developed the capacity to Be. Thus, because Being is constant, loving is constant. And loving as an expression of one's Being is constant, as is loving one's state of Being. Love is both, then: the product of one's Being *and* the first response to one's Being.

To Be so produces a quality of love that is neither present nor creatable on the third dimension of humanity's consciousness — yet this quality of love is being introduced as the heralding energy for loving in the Aquarian Age.

Loving Being — or to have a loving response to one's (newfound) capacity to Be — is beyond, and therefore not to be considered as or confused as self-love, for it is not. Self-love is a primary step toward the expression of love in relation to one's capacity to Be. But to Be, by its very act, links the universe to the soul to the self, to which link the self's response is love — not love for self, but love for the quality of Being that such connection creates.

Self-love is the response the ego feels when it is able to follow soul guidance and replace or transform unproductive actions with those that are more truthful, or powerful, or loving. Self-love thereby develops when an action the ego has perpetuated and *not* loved is replaced by one the ego does love.

This type of transformation, from soul to self, involves the purging of patterns the ego has been unable to love. Self-love develops, therefore, from transforming and replacing aspects of the self through soul-directed change.

Being, as well as loving Being, develops from capacities the universe bequeaths. For the universe to bequeath the capacity to Be requires that the individual's ego relinquish its need to create its own reality, because reality is the ego's interpretation of truth — and Being is in direct alignment with truth. The ego that is Being is neither able nor inclined to alter or edit that truth. Then, when the ego experiences the quality of life it can register in that mode, the response is unmistakably love. The ego loves Being.

With that loving response in place, the quality of love pouring through that human condition is beyond the vibration of love that pours from a self-love, even though self-love is not yet so abundant in the human condition. It is, however, the next level of love the human collective is aiming toward; and the love of Being is yet another level beyond that.

As a result, to love Being, and to direct that love into the human collective is, to some extent, an experiment without precedent, context or response — primarily because the vibration of such "love" passes through conditions in the human collective without finding any similar condition with which to exchange.

To love Being is far more refined a vibration than to love one's self. And, to love Being does automatically link any two or more like vibrations, irrespective of any three dimensional dissimilarities, incompatibilities or other such third dimensional evaluations.

To love Being brings two or more vibrations together because of a shared universal vibration. Thus, such individuals do not each love the other, per se, as is the collective three dimensional experience. The love they each experience merges them each with all the love the other experiences, as well as merging each with all the love all other similar vibrations experience. The resulting quantity and quality of love are, quite literally, beyond words; and that love feels, and indeed may at first be, beyond the human capacity to express.

That, too, is perfect, because this love is to Be, and only Be, for that *is* its fullest expression. And for it to Be in its fullest in each of the individuals capable of it is the universe's plan for registering the love of Being. Loving Being thereby commences the preparation for the Aquarian Age, wherein the exchange of such quality of love will be the creating principle for the quality of life and love which that fourth dimensional era will produce.

I realized that the the body is

like an antenna for God.

I could tune my body as a huge

cosmology of energies,

with lattices of light stretching

into other lattices of light.

Gradually I learned that there isn't

anything about our bodies

that is not an antenna,

this tuning fork for the divine.

— *Maya Angelou*

AN AFFIRMATION OF
AUTHENTIC SELF

by Maria Benning

I went to Boulder, Colorado for two weeks to help Dianne Lancaster put together her long overdue first book. Or so I thought that's why I went there. What I did in actuality, was participate in an intensive, accelerated course living the principles and guidelines contained herein. They are revolutionary in their promise of hope and transformation for the future.

Before I discovered Dianne's teachings, however, I had spent nearly half my life in depression, battling against the voice inside which continually told me, in its eerily seductive tone, to take my life. I marvel that I never gave in to the voice. In addition, I had within me a fearsome rage over which I had absolutely no control. I was its prisoner. Each time I spewed forth against those nearest and dearest to me, inevitably soon thereafter I lashed out at myself, physically and verbally, in my frustration and desperate desire to stop the hateful, hurtful behavior. Screaming in a pillow didn't stop the rage; cursing God didn't help; blaming my mother (father, husband, child, brother, friend) didn't end it either.

And yet today, three years after first hearing the terms, "the authentic vs. the adaptive self," "cosmic consciousness," "soul guidance," "transforming anger into love," and "truth *or* consequences," I can hardly recall feeling that deep sense of despair. I do remember it though, because I experienced it. There was no point to living, very little happiness in my day, and no hope of anything ever changing. It was a sad process leading toward a slow death. I thought for many years that my life would end, revealing no greater purpose . . .

. . . but I was wrong.

The guidelines contained in this book, and the enormous power of the additional included articles and instruments for awareness, provide the key to opening the door to a fulfilling, creative, joy-filled life. It is a life where truth has the strength to cut through the debilitating conditions that affect so many of us as individuals, and the planet as a whole. We need only open our eyes to see that the challenges facing humanity are greater than we, as individuals, can possibly reverse. What is needed is a quantum embracing of a system of values that will allow the changes in my life to impact you; for the changes you undergo to impact your neighbor; and for the changes your neighbor experiences to impact her community.

And so the rippling effect will continue. It requires each of us to begin producing these small shifts within ourselves in order to get the momentum going. And then, like waves reaching toward the shore, one after the other — we arrive.

Please *use* this information Dianne is teaching. It is truly the gift that keeps on giving. You will be thrilled, and sometimes brought to tears, by the metamorphosis that is unfolding.

ABOUT THE AUTHOR

 Dianne Lancaster, a business analyst and visionary, is president of 4•Sight Consulting Inc., a full-service business consulting firm located in Boulder, Colorado. With 24 years experience, its clients have included Fortune 500 companies, federal and state government agencies, small businesses, entrepreneurs, and individuals seeking investment and personal financial management counsel.

Dianne's Quantum Management Strategies, combined with her Management Imperatives approach to corporate wellness, offer a model for accessing and integrating the power of truth in business. In addition to numerous articles in business publications, she has written and lectured extensively on the economic times ahead, the risks and responsibilities of wealth in the 1990s, and the redistribution of power and money.

Among the workshop series Dianne teaches are "Women, Power, Money and Love," "Debt As A Spiritual Teacher," "The Spiritual Principles of Manifestation," and "The Role of World Servers in the Economic Times Ahead."

Combining macro- and micro-economic principles with the spiritual dimensions of entrepreneurship, Dianne has appeared on talk shows nationwide, emphasizing the economic, environmental and ethical challenges facing humanity's entry into the 21st century.

By employing the intuitive, soul-directed approach to business analysis, Dianne leads the 4•Sight team to view business situations from both the human and organizational perspectives. Knowing that some problems at work are brought from home, and that certain solutions must be directed there, 4•Sight assists employees, even their families, in reducing the types of stress and organizational dysfunction that manifest in the workplace. "To restore a company's confidence and potential, so that the company regains its power and enjoys renewed success," says Dianne, "is a meaningful, exhilarating experience."

The 4•Sight Consulting Team specializes in strategies for releasing untapped potential. Its strategies include management team building, corporate values assessment, ethics review, synthesis between personal and business needs, and personal and business ethics.

ORDER FORM

Reclaiming the Authentic Self

_____   Number of copies @ $14.95 each = $ _____ total for books

Plus sales tax (7.3%) for Colorado   _____

Plus shipping   _____

($5.00 each–Priority Mail;

$3.00 each–book rate)

                                   $ _____ **TOTAL**

Mail To:

Name _____

Address _____

City _____ State _____ Zip _____

❑ Check   ❑ M.O.   ❑ Visa   ❑ MC

Name _____

_____ Exp. Date _____

Thank You!

Coming Soon

Dear 4•Sight Press: Please send information on your upcoming books:

❑ The Karmic Corporation
❑ Women, Power, Money and Love
❑ Debt As a Spiritual Teacher
❑ The Role of World Servers in the Redistribution of Power and Wealth
❑ Aquarian Numerology™ and Tarot
❑ The Aquarian Agents™ Handbook
❑ Reclaiming the Body Beautiful

4•Sight Press Inc, P. O. Box 1488, Boulder, CO 80306-1488
Phone: (303) 545-2216 • Fax: (303) 545-9259